THE VIEW FROM NOW

The Teachers With

Lauren Granger

AirPropel Books

AIRPROPEL

THE VIEW FROM NOW

LAUREN C. GRANGER

For reproduction permission, contact publisher

AirPropel Books

LaurenCGranger.com lauren@laurengranger.com

Printed in the United States of America
First Printing 2018
ISBN 978-0-9981784-2-4
Library of Congress Control Number: 2018908309
Cover Design by Mauricio Vilches

TABLE OF CONTENTS

ACKNOWLEDGEMENTS

It is with tremendous gratitude that I acknowledge and give thanks for helpers with this book. The task of creating a book is grand and much more than I could do by myself. For technical support I'm grateful for Flavio Vilches, for editing, Deborah Ward, and for the exceptional cover design, my thanks go out to Mauricio Vilches.

SIDE NOTES TO LAUREN, THE READERS, AND ALL WHO WILL PARTICIPATE

A NOTE TO THE READERS FROM THE TEACHERS

"It is with joy that we continue to send messages of love through our writings. The whole world will eventually unite because of the messages that we give to you. Now is your turn to do your part."

A NOTE TO LAUREN FROM THE TEACHERS

"Now keep writing, talking, and sharing the messages. We understand that you have physical duties, but when at all possible, put the messages first. Understand that this is your mission, you purpose, your job. Others cannot do what you were sent to do."

A NOTE FROM LAUREN TO THE TEACHERS

"I'll keep writing but just saying that I want to better understand. How did people get so lost? Were humans always detached from spirit knowledge? And I'm having a difficult time understanding Jesus' crucifixion. I can't understand such badness and such goodness in one place. I look forward to the day when the cross is no longer a symbol of Jesus."

THE TEACHERS RESPONSE

"The day will come when the crosses are removed along with the ideas of sin. A loving world is unfolding. Rejoice."

THE VIEW FROM NOW

INTRODUCTION

This final book of the NOW series, will be about peace and discovery. You will be discovering another path for maintaining Earth. We will be talking about it.

You see, the old paths are outdated. It is time for a refresher. We will be talking about the new VIEW FROM NOW The view will begin with many changes and progress to a state of peaceful equilibrium. Expect the beginning to look like turmoil. Expect the end to look peaceful. Earth is in transition now. The changes have begun. We want everyone to know of this new coming; this new way of being.

There has been much said about my (Jesus) next coming. I can tell you now that it will be when there is peace on Earth. You all will be the peacekeepers. You all will pave the path. It will be your contributions that save Earth. You have the messages; you have always known the path. Now, people of Earth will walk the path to freedom and peace. This will be done together as one planet. Everyone will agree that the common good of one is good for all. There is no other way.

The new world leaders, not the politicians, will be guiding everyone to a peaceful existence.

It is time to know that the choices are yours. All the paths have been laid. The direction is clear. Do you want a peaceful Earth or do you prefer the excitement and thrill of chaos? I'll continue to talk about peace, yet if chaos is your choice, it is yours for the taking.

The beauty of a peaceful planet is that everyone will experience it. Instead of little pockets of peace and pockets of non-peace, everyone will be sharing the same experience of abundance, love, joy, and health. All the physical and spiritual desires will be available to everyone. We think the desires are worth striving for. The new path will be paved for all. The elite and the beggar will become equals. Everyone will have enough. Try to imagine the new way of being. It is coming.

As we have said, other planets already live this way; in health and abundance, in love and joy. Now Earth, it is your turn.

We'll talk now about time in space. Be aware that earth people are not doomed to stay on earth. There is a vast, infinite, foreverland available to you all- and to others on different planets. In the future, there will be more togetherness amongst all. Can you image inviting friends from another planet to your outdoor barbecue? Does that bring about a smile? We hope so. Preparations are being made for peaceful visits. Be assured, and know perfectly well that first, Earth will learn to live in peaceful harmony. Know for sure that no one will want to be a part of your science fiction creations. All visitors will come when there is peace. We will tell you about this now, so that you may know. Future generations will have these experiences. Your great grandchildren will be enjoying the visits and the travel. In a world of infinite time, a few generations are a very short time. For now, begin learning the ways of a peaceful planet.

THE VIEW FROM NOW

PART ONE

A FEW MESSAGES FROM JESUS

And now, the process of peace will begin. You see, everyone has the connection to peace. And everyone is a part of the infinite, god, source, whole, etc. We understand that most people have not known about your connection or didn't know how to connect. I WANT TO MAKE VERY CLEAR THAT YOUR GOD IS NOT A MAN IN A FAR AWAY PLACE. Can't you see how mankind created this likeness of Homo-sapiens to represent a god? And mankind gave both loving and fearful attributes to this created god. Can you see that this creation was to keep people of earth behaving in a particular way? This belief lacks freedom. Therefore, it is restricting and judgmental. Pure love does none of this. Pure love is a part of everyone, every plant and every animal. The energy of love is the energy of life. One is equal to the other. If you want to find the rule maker, look inside you. That is where the answers are. Now you know. Don't be looking towards a man-made creation with limitations and judgments. I, Jesus, never told you or anyone that your answers of how to live will come from a faraway god. I, Jesus, told you all that love is the only answer. Love will set you free. Infinite love is a part of all. Infinite love is what you are looking for. Yes, it is out there, but it is also within. Infinite love is the energy of life; the highest clearest frequency available. Infinite love does not judge, limit, or separate. Are you getting my message now? The power of god is within you. It is an energy. It is not the likeness of a human man who lives in a secluded place. Love does not have a judgment day. Do you understand? This may take time for some of you to believe. The old beliefs were well cemented. The new beliefs aren't cemented at all. The new beliefs are infinite rays of pure energy. With that being said, tune in to your loving self and share from your place of love. Know that you don't need to be forgiven for having earthly experiences. When you die, or as some say, transcend the body, you will not be judged. You will be loved before, during, and after this earthly experience.

Now that some of the facts have been set straight, let's continue.

I'm going to let you know about my experiences on Earth and as a spiritual being. You all can have similar experiences. You see, I am not your god. I am for now in spiritual form but have lived in physical embodiment.

Such a big deal was made about my last incarnation. True, I created a ruckus with the ways of society. True, I was a rebel and a revolutionist. I rebelled against established ideas of greed, judgments, status, and dominance. My truth, then and now, is that everyone is equal and valuable in the eyes of love. I and many others were willing to die for this message. People are still being killed for promoting peaceful beliefs. In that sense, you can say that I and many others died for you- for your enlightenment. But we did not die for your sins. In the eyes of love, there is no such thing as sin. Can you understand this? I hope so. It is time to get the message of love, and to stop talking about sins. This is a beginning; a good place to start with the message of love. Hear me now. When you commit a crime to yourself or another, you are not a sinner; you are living from a place outside of your loving self. You can talk about crimes towards each other; I prefer to talk about love towards each other. The amount of love towards each other will equal the amount of love you feel for yourself. When you kill another, you are not experiencing the love within yourself. When you judge others, you are not living from your loving self. Do you understand that you cannot express loving kindness when you are experiencing negative thoughts and emotions? What I want to tell everyone is that living from your place of loving connection is the answer to everything.

Living from your loving self *is* your connection to everything. This doesn't seem so difficult to understand. Now that Earth is entering a stage of enlightenment, people will begin to understand. This is good news. Yet, there will be resistance from some. Mostly from those who are unwilling to give up their power and position. Let it be for now. Know that love will absorb resistance.

And now, it is time for you to know that the way of peace is through the way of your connection. That means, connect to the "good" part of you. Connect to the part of you that makes you happy, joyful, silly, fun and loving. Spend most of your time in that place. The more time you spend there, the less stress, anger, depression, illness, and chaos you will experience. That sounds reasonable and easy, yet I know that it is not. Choosing your energy frequencies will take time and practice. The more you do this the easier it will become. Do this no matter what your life situation may be at any particular time. Practice during the difficult times as well as during the easy times. As I have said, when the easy times are with you, give gratitude. Gratitude is an energy frequency. Use it to create an easier life.

Know that you don't have to participate in negative energy frequencies. Know that believing in yourself, and learning to love your self will end most negative energy. For all you caregivers, the most important lesson you can teach is self-love. Teach that everyone is connected to infinite love. Teach that while in self-love forgiving others is easy. Forgiving others will come naturally when you are experiencing self-love. With self-love, there is no contest. Through the eyes of self-love can be seen that everyone is equal. Love yourself so that you can love each other. Teach others to love themselves so that they can love each other. Infinite love for self will become infinite love for others. That is a game changer.

Now, it is also time to know that you are important. Your energy is necessary for creating the growth and expansion of the energy of earth. Let me clarify by saying that your positive energy is necessary. Your negative energy reduces growth. At the cost of repetition and redundancy I will continue to say, you are the continuation and creator of all that is. It is your positive energy that feeds the energy of always. That is why you are in physical body. That is your purpose. Your purpose is filled through your acts of joy, kindness, love, and celebrations. In time, this will be easy. People won't feel the disparity that is present now. It is your job now to become aware of your energy frequencies and to choose those which work best for you and for all. Even- and most importantly, in times of inner conflict choose the highest frequencies. In all times, aim for positive high frequencies. It takes practice along with conscious awareness. The view is of peaceful existence; the time is now.

IN THE BEGINNING, IN LIGHT AND DARK

Now we will talk about the creation of all. The creation of time. There *was* a time of darkness. There *was* a time of very little life. And the life of that time was mostly unimportant except for creating more life. So it did. The small amount of mostly insignificant life re-created. As it grew, so did the light, and the nurturing. The life began learning how to care for life. This was way before time was measured. As you know, eventually, life advanced. Here you are. The darkness of life which does very little for producing life is still available. The loving side of life, which is the light and nurturing side, is also available. The loving side = life. Do you understand this? It is energy frequencies. Love is life. It is that simple. Without love = death. This is broken down for you so that you can better understand the path you are on. All of you have moments of love and lovelessness in you; otherwise, known as the light and the dark, the good and the bad. You are both. Everyone is. When you incarcerate the bad person, you also incarcerate the good person. Is that what you meant to do? The message in this is for you to become aware and direct your flow of energy. Your energy will flow towards more life or towards more non-life. Become conscious of the energy that you use; the energy of life and the energy of non-life. As you become conscious, future generations will be affected by your energy. It's best to choose now. Every frown and every smile, every word of love and every word of hate will make a difference in infinite time. Become enlightened about your choices, your moments, and your actions.

CHANGE FOR ALL IN DUE TIME

Planet earth is in transition. Most likely, you can't see the transition. Those who were alive during the age of enlightenment, or the dark ages, or the industrial revolution, probably weren't able to step out and look in at the whole picture of change. The same is true for this revolution of peace. But hundreds of years from now, the changes will be evident. Some people of earth are aware and are living differently because of this change. Others will never see it, never be aware, and never change in one life time. Still all moves in the direction of peace.

It is understandable that those who don't understand or know of the change will not be participating. In time, everyone will participate. In time, every rebirth or re-entry into the physical world will be living with more of the change towards peace. The movement is on. For those of you who understand, we ask for your patience and understanding with the ones who aren't yet aware. There is a correct time for everyone. We don't expect a take-over of ideas and believes. We expect the change to happen for everyone in due time. We say this in the hopes of eliminating arrogance. Everyone's time is for a reason. There will always be the front of a line, and the end of the line. Both are necessary to make the line. The line will form a circle, and then disperse when the time is right. Think of it as energy with various colors moving towards expansion. Your purpose is to love everyone in every position of the change to peace. Can you do this? We think that you can. Time is on your side.

We want to talk about the possibilities, the ongoing, and the reactions to change. You see, this revolution to peace is going to happen with a lot of change. The change will begin internally with one person and then another until eventually everyone has changed to the ways of peace. My suggestion is that you not focus on the goings on outside of yourself. Each person will be going on with their lives in their own way. It is best to focus on the changes which will be happening in you. When we say "focus" we mean to create awareness. We do not mean to begin mental manipulations. Don't make it difficult. Simply become aware. That is all. Notice and let go.

Of course, there is always time for reflection. Time to reflect on the comings and goings of life in the physical realm. These reflections are an opportunity of growth. Enjoy the reflections as they appear. Take time to ponder, reflect, and expand. These are true moments of joyful rebuilding. Enjoy.

It is with much joy that we experience the movement towards peace. You see, the time is here and now. The movement is in place. We tell you this so as to encourage participation. The sooner you start participating, the more joyful you will be. For each participant, there will be many changes of beliefs, and behaviors. The change will be gradual in everyone. Practice. Continue to accept these words and practice living a life of inner peace. Let it be. Begin now.

THE NEW OLD WORLD
We will now talk about the beginning of a new world. In this new world, which is really the same old world with new experiences

of joy, will be the final development into a peaceful planet. Once this happens, a range of new opportunities will be presented. The new opportunities will further the development of life on an infinite plane. The scope and meaning of life will be clearer to everyone. The contributions of each life form will become more significant as each life becomes more centered towards its purpose. There will be much less wasted energy. Once the negative energy which is presently experienced on earth has been reduced, the positive energy will be more productive for all of earth and your universe. This is exciting news. This is exciting because the time has come for peace and joy on Earth. Finally!

TAKE A LOOK BEFORE YOU CREATE

And now we will talk about the joys of peace. We are aware of your turbulent lives and past histories. The time is now to let go. Stop carrying the sword and shield of evil, bad, fear, negative energy. It is time to put down your weapons of words. It is time to look at alternatives. Now is a good time to look at a view of peace instead of looking at the view of hurt and revenge or depression. It is your choice and all you need to know is within you. Visualize that which you expect to create. Feel the joy and create it from within. This always puts you in power. Waiting for others to create your joy will most likely not create the life you desire. *You* have the power to create your joy. Use it. Visualize and experience your joy in order for joy to manifest.

Now, we suggest that you support each other in the quest for inner peace. We suggest that you talk about the peace you see coming from others. Talk about the peace coming from yourself; as much as possible, stop the babble of negative energy. That is to say separate the event from the drama. Events, both positive and negative will happen. The long term drama then becomes an event of its own. There is no need to build a separate dramatic event of negative energy. It serves no useful purpose. Release and surrender. Allow peace to take the place of negative babble.

Are you willing? Are you ready to allow? You see peace is here, it is available. The reason it has not spread is because people aren't allowing it to spread. People aren't breathing into peace. There are plenty of moments to practice and plenty of moments to create and accept peace. There are plenty of moments to let go of struggle. We suggest that you begin choosing these moments. We suggest that you practice awareness of the moments. Pick a time, a moment and begin. Begin with the awareness of your power; end with awareness of your peaceful creation. Begin Now.

THE ADVENTUROUS JOURNEY TO YOUR LOVING SELF

Now we will talk about the beginning of a new era. The time has come for a change in the direction to loving self. We want you to know that you are the hope for planet Earth. You are the key to survival. YOU, each and every one of you are the hope and the direction of a surviving planet. It is your energy frequencies that will propel this planet into the future. The future of Earth depends on the positive energy from its life forms. Are you understanding this? Let me repeat. The survival of Earth depends on the positive energy of its life forms. Positive energy frequencies are growth and expansion. Negative energy frequencies lead towards death and destruction. Your planet, your choice. To choose life, start with yourself. Start with loving yourself, being happy with yourself, and being joyful. For many, this will have to be learned. Many of you were not shown love and haven't developed self-love. I tell you that love is within each of you. Everyone is connected to infinite love. Everyone can find that connection and live from that place. No matter what your experiences have been, you are attached to infinite love. Release the pile of negative energy. Find the inherent right to your infinite loving attachment to all that is. Now this is a journey worth pursuing; the adventurous journey to your loving self.

The amazement comes from the light of love which you will experience once you reach the place of your self-love connection to infinite love. Amazing. That is to say, once you have gotten rid of all your negative debris, will be the amazing experience of inner love. Much more thrilling than a roller-coaster ride, or a sky-dive is the amazement, the feeling, the power of your love.

And so begins the journey to one-ness. All the separate life forms are connected by the frequency of love. Again, let's call it HEF-high energy frequency. Your word for the highest energy frequency is love. It is your connection to all of life... and your entire planet is alive. Everyone, every animal, every mineral is connected to the life form of high energy frequency- HEF. Infinite Love is your connection to all that is. Does this make sense to you? If so, then you will know to continue the expansion of HEF – Love. Direct it to your entire planet. Direct it to all the animals. Direct it from your connection to infinite love. No, you don't have to physically embrace the poisonous snake or spider. We are asking you to understand that the snake and the spider are connected to the same life force as you. Respect all connections to infinite love – to HEF. Even the cockroach sustains life on Earth with its connection to high energy frequencies. Its wish to survive is driven by its connection to the highest energy frequency. Now you can understand why the cockroach runs for shelter when a person turns on the light in the middle of the night.

The connection to the highest energy frequency, HEF, infinite love, is invisible and to some, unknown yet, it is knowable. Infinite love can be recognized, experienced and shared. Your journey, your path to infinite love is short, yet it may take years or life times. The path is no longer than your willingness to connect to what is already a part of you. The willingness includes a desire to remove mountains of suffering, and disbelief, which came from low energy frequencies. LEFs is the darkness which does not produce life. Low energy, short range negative energy, hate, fear judgment, greed... decreases life on Earth. That is the truth. The color of the auras surrounding you and your planet reflect the energy you are producing. Choose to spend most of your time in high energy frequency. With practice, this will become easier. Now is a good time to practice.

LIVING BOTH YOUR SEPARATION AND YOUR TOGETHERNESS

Let's talk about the ideas of separation and togetherness. We, the we of you and me, are all a part of one mass energy. This mass energy is what some of you know as God. Others call it love, the whole, infinite source.... Without a name, it is still the energy of life; the energy that sustains forever. The connection belongs to everyone in spirit and in body. The separate energy pieces in the spiritual realm also belong to the energy of life. Individual spiritual energies are separate from each other yet all are connected. The same is true within the physical realm. Each physical identity is separate from another, yet all are connected to the same life force. This is good to know. You can see that separation and togetherness exists in all of forever. It just depends on the depth of your view. We suggest that you look at the view with more than a human eye. With the eye and other physical senses you can experience separateness. That is to say that you can see, hear, taste, smell, and touch differences that separate one from another. Hay does not smell like pepper. Hay and pepper are physically separate yet they both came from and contain the same seeds of forever. They both contain a connection to life, love, god energy source. It can be no other way. The other way would be of non-energy, void, non-existence. Because hay and pepper exist, they came from the energy of all that is. So did you. So did I. Are you understanding that we are all in this together? In our separate ways, we all are together in the creation of all that is. You are creating. Take a look at your creations. Understand that the physical you is connected to the non-physical you. Your non-physical self is actually seeable but not from your view. Just as you can't see a proton neither can you see your connection to the whole. The proton still exists in everything. So too, does the high energy frequency of life exist in everything. Now, live your life from both your separation and your togetherness.

We can tell you that it's in the energy of life that all exists- the energy that you can't see. We want you to become acquainted with this energy. First become acquainted, and then begin to use it. After all, it is a part of you and available for you to use in your physical "seeable" life on Earth. This energy of life which you call love, source, god... is the missing part of your separate physical existence. It is not really missing, but just invisible to your sense of sight, sound, taste, touch. To tune in to this part of you, stop using your physical eyes, ears, nose... and don't process through your physical brain. Instead, get as quiet as possible and without distractions. A good time is as you fall asleep or as you begin to wake. Other good times are when you are doing rote, repetitive, mindless, activities. Practice. Go into "nothingness" and hear everything. Go into a zombie state and have a conversation with all of time. Ask questions. Get used to day dreaming. Know that eternal life will talk with you. The visions of forever are available. Practice. The child knows how to do this. The young child can see and hear on both sides. Some of you will get this, some of you won't. Some of you will listen in your daydreams, and in your hours before and after sleep. Some of you will learn to ask questions and listen for answers. Practice awareness. Start with believing. Allow the peace of quiet time. Occasionally connect with your foreverness.

A REVOLUTIONARY IDEA OF PEACE

And now, it is time to re-think a revolutionary idea. The idea is that all of Earth will be at peace. We know this is hard for some of you to accept. Some of you don't want to accept peace. Some of you want to argue, fight, judge... so be it. Just know that the future of Earth will be of peace. Also know that peace is not difficult to obtain. All it takes is desire from one person, then another until everyone desires peace. The beginning of Earth was, and the end of Earth will be- in peace. Know this as a truth. Expect the time of love and joy to arrive. Expect happiness and celebration. Now is a good time to begin. As often as possible, live with happiness. Your circumstances will then begin to shift and align with your high energy. Live in love and joy. Allow it to be no matter what your situation. Create the situation of your choice. Create love and joy. Your situations will begin to align with your positive energy. The changes will take some time. Best to not focus on your negative energy. The negative energy will dissipate by itself when you focus on positive energy.

SALVATION AND REDEMPTION

Now it is time to hear about the coming of salvation; the coming of you being saved. That means your own salvation in your own time while here on earth. The salvation of your existence while in physical body is determined by you. The salvation that we speak of is not from your "evil" acts. The salvation is the shift from negative energy to positive energy. The salvation is from guilt, anger, sadness, jealousy, fear, greed... to love. It is that simple. You are your own savior. Your power comes from within. It does not come from other people. Your power comes from your willingness to believe in love- self-love, infinite love. Your power comes from living joyfully from your spirit. There is your salvation, your redemption, your blessing, your godliness. Go forth in your salvation, your belief in your power of goodness and your power of love.

THE TIME OF EVOLVING

It is a wonderful great new day. Let us begin by talking about the time for all things. From our view of endless time, we see the beginnings, the transitions, and the completions. It is at this time that we talk about the completion of "Project Earth." That is to say that Earth has gone full circle into its wholeness. From our view, we can see the beginning of Earth and its transitions into peacefulness. Earth is ready to align with other planets that have completed the process. All planets evolve within their own time. They are born, they transition, they complete. You can view Earth as peacefully moving in space. Visualize, and see in your mind's eye the peaceful movement of Earth amongst the galaxies and solar systems of an infinite universe. Gone is the time of struggle to survive. Even though we view this end of transitioning, we understand that your short physical life span will not see the outcome of the transition. This will take a few more generations, which means more or less another few hundred years; a very short time in the whole of all that is. We say this so that you understand what you cannot see. You cannot see the peacefulness of future earth, yet you are now creating the path. It is NOW that people on Earth are processing the changes to peace. It is now that the path is being laid. As all planets evolve in their own time, so does the physical life of plants and animals evolve individually. The human life of planet Earth is evolving into peace. When you are ready for the View, you will see it. Once you see it, align with the view of peace. Align with others who also see the view of peace. Be patient with those who are not ready. Don't judge them. Accept that in good time Earth will evolve into peace.

Now, is the time to talk about the encroaching awareness of change. It is with deep gratitude that we express our joy for those of you who came forward in human physical form to create the movement of peace on earth.

Now, we will talk about the laws and rules of expanding peace. The process begins with a thought energy which becomes a belief which becomes an action. It starts with "I can" or "I will." Believe in your ability to contribute. Focus on *your* ability. Know that you have the ability. All that is necessary is for you to create desire. With practice, it shouldn't be that difficult.

You are on the right track. Keep building momentum. Keep singing in the shower, smiling at others as you pass by, reaching out a hand in greeting. Of course your words count greatly. Keep in mind that thoughts are non-verbal words. Talk about the good stuff, look for the good stuff, and visualize the good stuff. Look for the positive. Look for what could go right instead of what could go wrong. Become conscious of where you are directing your energy. Stay on the path of peace. Above all else be true to your connection to all that is. Be true to your connection to the whole. You *are* connected to the greatest truths. Through this connection you will expand the energy, the life of all Earth. Live in peace, walk in peace. Go forward now, in peace.

HOW TO LISTEN WITHIN
We will move now to the energy of time. Timeless energy. A source that is infinite. We think of it as love. Many of you think of it as god. The name doesn't matter. Without the word, the energy is the same. It is the highest frequency of positive energy; the all and the forever. No need to look for anything more or anything deeper. Look into your connection to all that is.

Rejoice with knowing that you are an extension of forever; past, present, future, and that you will not, nor will anyone else "poof" and disappear into nothing. When your spirit energy releases its current body, the spirit will still exist as a unit of the larger part of all. Rejoice, celebrate, and live it up!

Now many of you ask how to connect with the deeper part of you. Well, you are already connected; all you need to do is listen within instead of "with-out." Listening "with-out" means using your ears to hear all the sounds in your physical world. Listening with-in means developing the ability to listen to the voices that aren't in the physical world. This is somewhat like meditation. When one is "thinking" one is listening to an inner voice. Allow that "thinking" inner voice to speak. Ask it questions, give it a topic. Get personal with questions. Are you always with me, can you give direction, do you have a name, how long have you been helping me? Just start up a dialogue. Get used to hearing the different types of answers or feelings. Get used to listening within. Practice. Trust. Believe. Eventually, you might start recognizing the difference between you and them. Enjoy the meet-ups.

SEE THE CONFLICT AS A PATH TO PEACE

Now is a good time to focus on the differences between wealth and poverty; too much and not enough, sickness and health, maintenance and prosperity, illusion and truth. The real truth is that the cost of too much and too little is out of balance. The need to equalize is necessary for the existence of Earth.

Let us begin by saying that now is a perfectly good time to make assessments. Assess the benefits, the flow, and the rationale behind your attitudes that separate.

It is a good time to look at a view of equality. Let us paint the picture. When life on Earth survives the negative energy, the view will be of peace. All along the goal has been getting to peace- for everyone. Peace doesn't come when some have and others don't have. When peace comes to everyone, it will look like an explosion of light in the heavens. It *will* be explosions of light in positive energy frequencies. Other planets will receive the messages of peace on Earth. This will be a glorious time of celebration. Be assured, the event of peace is coming.

When you view all the chaos in the world, know that it will resolve into peace. Know that the chaos is necessary for bringing to light, an awareness of inequalities. Poverty and greed will balance. So will sickness and health. From the paintings of chaos will emerge the scenes of peace. Visualize, imagine, and know that Earth is on the path of peace.

Again, be reminded that this time of chaos is not to be feared. You will be better off to understand and to participate in the coming of peace. Whenever possible, step out of the picture and view from a distance. See that changes are being made. See the positive result. See peace.

THE REALITY OF REAL TRUTH
Today we will talk about the ups and downs and sideways of reality. Wow, alternate realities. There is a reality that is a logical stream of occurrences and creations. Then there is an assumed reality about the factual reality. It is easy to understand, and through the years (thousands) the assumed truths became the accepted. We know that it will be difficult to undo all the beliefs. It will be much easier for each person to challenge their own beliefs in a search for truth. Many of you are already on this search. We are pleased. Others need a shakeup, a wake up. This will happen in many ways. Core beliefs, are only true until the person releases them. The old belief or assumed

truth is released when knew information is introduced and believed. This is a time for new truths and new beliefs.

It is time to search. It is time to challenge your beliefs. It is time to challenge the message givers. It is important to update the messages. Some of the old messages about me, Jesus, about what I said or did are incorrect. Now is a good time to straighten the record. Really, there is only one thing you need to believe and that is in the power you have of the highest energy frequency which people on Earth call love. Believe that the power resides inside of you. The power is not outside- in another person or entity. Your power did not and does not reside in me. I am not your power. I am your guide who leads you to the message of loving peace. Don't worship me. Instead, align with the truth which is a part of who you are. The best way to be aligned with me, Jesus, is to align with your spirit, your truth within. If you want to worship me, then worship you. If you want to follow me, then follow your truth within. It is from within that you will be brought into enlightenment. It is from within that you will pass through stages of growth which lead you to the peace you seek.

The enlightenment you seek is a higher energy plane. Everyone is welcome and everyone will arrive. Everyone will take this journey in their own time. Everyone will let go of the dark, lower energy, shorter wave lengths and move up to the lighter, higher energy. The lower frequencies are where depression, murder, fear, greed, jealousy, etc. gets its feed. If you are a person working through lower frequencies, you will find the light and the path within your heart-spirit. Your time in dark energy is limited. You are free to move up whenever you choose. Start with believing that the energy of love runs through you. Look for it, connect with it. You are not doomed to a belief based in some sort of misery. Start with challenging your beliefs. The more you believe in you and the love within you, the more of what you seek will appear. Opportunities will begin to appear when you believe in your connection to the highest of all that is. You are connected to the *Real truth.*

JUDGMENT IS NOT A PART OF THE LARGER PURPOSE

A good thing to know is that there is time for all wounds to heal. Wherever, whenever a negative energy interrupted your life, there is time to release the energy and replace it with a positive. Always- and always- it is your choice to hold on to the negative or replace it with a positive. Always. Do you get the idea of always there is positive energy available to you. Always, it is your choice to accept it. Keep in mind that always is an infinite time. You are an infinite being. So is the person you don't like, or the person whom you don't understand, or.... You are all on the same path. Stop the judgment. Know that you are all one with each other because you are all on the path of life and positive energy. Each person is experiencing their own path in their own time. All paths will merge as one. Stop judging, start loving. Begin to accept that which you cannot understand. Accept differences on the path. Accept positive and negative energy on the path. Accept that you are on the same path as them. Some are in front of you, some are behind you. Love is the glue that binds each and all together. Practice love.

It is a good time to know about your future. You see, the time has come to evolve into a higher energy planet. It is now that this is happening. It is now that changes are being made. We are saying this so that everyone can become aware of the changes and the paths to enlightenment and peace. It is now that the people on planet Earth have come forward to represent the changes. You did this for the larger purpose of expanding positive energy. Each of you chose to re-enter at this time, to bring about the change. The role you are playing is necessary for the whole. Your individual roles bring awareness. Those whom you like and those whom you don't like are all bringing you

18

awareness of positive and negative energy. With this awareness, choices will be made. Think about it. Choose peace. Create peace while amongst negative energy. Let go of judgments and see a larger purpose. Act on a larger purpose. Become the larger purpose.

SEEING GOODNESS OR BADNESS

The time has come to enjoy one another. Enjoy the goodness in each person. It is there. Goodness is a part of everyone. Look for it in everyone. You will see the goodness in them when you are attached to the goodness in you. It works both ways. When you see the "badness" in them, you are looking through your own lens of "badness." Best thing to do when this happens is to become aware, then change course. Become aware of what you see and what you experience in others. With awareness, comes a choice. You can choose to stay in negative energy or choose to see the goodness. Practice! The more goodness you see, even in people with "bad" behavior, the more goodness will become a part of your life. We think you want goodness in your life. Recognize it everywhere and it will be reflected back to you.

Now, the time has come to look for goodness everywhere. Have a search party. Really! Create search parties with people who are also looking for the goodness. Then talk about what you find. Talk about it in the media, in your group gatherings, and at one-on-ones. The more you look for goodness, and then talk about it, the more goodness you will be creating for yourself and for planet Earth. Practice Now. Change your view now. View the greatness in everyone. You have the choice.

BEGINNING YOUR JOURNEY TO PEACE

It is time to talk again about the beginning of the end. Talk again about the time when people of planet Earth will create a sustainable planet. The time is here for the end of negative energy and the beginning of living in peace. As we have said, both energies will always be available but the time has come to live with peaceful high frequencies. This is a wake-up call. People of Earth will have the benefit of living peacefully like many other planets. It is time. We are pleased to announce the coming of peace on earth. You are the peace makers. The peace does not come from a mysterious force in the unknown. It comes from you and your connection to the whole of all that it. It comes from the high energy frequencies- the highest, purist is what you call love. Infinite love.

Your change of heart, change of direction, change of path can take a long time- if not a life time. Begin Now. Begin by understanding that you have nothing to lose and much to gain. Begin by making a habit of seeing the good in life, then talking about it. See, hear, feel the goodness. Share it with others.

THE VIEW OF LOVE

Let's go to the stars. Let's look at the moon. Let's experience Earth from space. That is our view. We, your teachers can see Earth from space. You can too. It takes a willingness to imagine and go in your mind. We invite you to come with us and view your planet. Your planet is alive. That we can tell from far far away. We see its aura. We see its gasses, which are energies. We see the energy of love. Imagine. Can you see it too? We know that love=life. That is how we know that planet Earth is alive. We share this view with you in hopes of keeping Earth alive. That is up to you; each of you. The energy you create will make the difference of life or death. Oh, maybe you don't consciously choose death. But when you act with negative energy, the energy of death will be on Earth. This energy creates illness, disease, famine.... We also see the negative energy from our view in space. We see the aura of destruction.

What do you see? How are you contributing to your view? The time is now to choose a vision and create it.

We want you all to see the beauty, the love. We aren't just making small talk. We want you to greatly understand. It is our plan to create in everyone, beautiful awareness of eternal, infinite love. It is our plan to create messages of love. All you have to do is tune in. Listen and look for the messages of love They are all around you, yet it is your choice to tune into high energy frequencies of love, or low energy frequencies of fear. Whichever you tune to will become. At any time you can begin to close your eyes and ears to that which is of no value to planet earth. When you hear any sound of separation, hatred, greed violence- don't tune in. If not fed, low energy frequency will become silent. When you hear sounds of oneness, togetherness, joy, peace, tune in; pick up the energy and move with it. March in the revolution of peace. The best way to silence negative energy is to not listen. The best way to expand positive energy is to pick up the beat and become one with your internal connection to the greatest energies of all.

This is a simple program to save life on earth. In all its simplicity, practice is required. Practice a willingness to remove the old tapes in your beliefs. Practice building new beliefs with images and sounds of loving beauty. Talk about it; share the beauty that you hold within. Begin now.

YOUR HIGHEST PURPOSE
It is time to understand the purpose of your being on Earth. We have explained that you are here to move energy. You have physical mass and the ability to manipulate the energy far into space. We ask that you take this seriously. Seriously means joyfully. Understand that you are manipulating energy with and

without your knowing. We want you to become aware and manipulate with purpose. With awareness comes choices. Choose to experience the energy frequencies of love, joy, happiness etc. That is what we ask you to consider. This is another wake-up call. This is a time of higher awareness. When you have awakened to higher awareness, share the word. Talk about it with others who may not read these words. Don't preach about love and joy. Simply become love and joy. As you do, others will notice. That is the best way to share the message; living from your higher self- your joyful self. You *can* change the world; one smile at a time. One smile, one handshake, one hug, one laughter becomes life changing events. It is time for world peace and you are a peacemaker. Begin now. Create from your connection to all that is. That is your highest purpose.

We will talk about the time it takes to create change. This can be done instantly or it can take many life times. There is a time of readiness in each of you. Readiness comes with awareness. Become aware of your potential and your power. Know that you have the ability to create a peaceful, loving, thriving planet. This is your turn because you are in body. Make the best use of this time. Become peaceful and loving. With all the situations and events on Earth, each of you is in a place to create change. Wherever you are and no matter what is going on in your life, you are in a position to love. Understand that there is no better time and no better place. Excuses aren't necessary- love, joy, and understanding is necessary.

THE YOU AND US TEAM
Today we will talk about the differences between you and me. You the physical and me the spiritual.

In the beginning of formation, all of life was energy. Actually, it still is, just more diversified. Energy began taking different forms. You see, energy has the ability to change into whatever force is pulled upon it. Energy can be considered fluid with its ability to change. Energy has no "mind" of its own. It can't say, "I'm going to do this or that." Energy acts and reacts to the force of other energies. You could say that energies create a dance with each other. It is really beautiful and interesting to watch. We tell you this so that you realize your power. When energy began separating into different forms, the different forms began pulling energy towards or away from itself. Over time, forms developed more clearly. Let's jump forward to the forms of present day humans. You have the ability to draw towards you and other humans, a sustainable life force. By doing so, you would be assuring the survival of humans. The energy of survival is what you call infinite love, self-love, love of others or merely love. We don't call it love although we know to what you refer. We think of it as pure positive energy. The energy of sustainable life is the energy that you call love.

Now, back to the differences between *you* and *us; w*e are all forms of humans- just with different powers. Because we in spiritual form are without bodies, it is much easier for us to see the larger picture. We can be omnipotent on many levels including planet Earth and beyond. We can understand your desires, your wishes, your emotions, your thoughts. You can think of us as a loving extension of yourself. We are present to help you, to serve you, to guide you. We do not judge as that would serve no purpose. It is our pleasure to help you find peace and happiness.

You, on the other hand, are in body with the purpose of moving energy. You chose to do this. No one decided for you, and no one else chose for you to re-enter physical form. The energy that you choose to move is up to you. All the energies both positive and negative, high frequency and low frequency are available to you.

No matter what your circumstances, you still have a choice of the energy you draw to you. ALWAYS.

Now let's start working together. In the face of perceived hell, your mind or your brain probably doesn't have all the answers. We see the problem, the concern and a more clear answer. The smartest thing you can do is breathe into your spirit self, your infinite loving self, your connection to all that is. Sometimes you call this your heart. We don't recognize it as a body part. You might think of it more as an umbilical cord to infinite all. That is where you will find us in spirit form. We will be leading, guiding, and encouraging you to a greater truth and a greater peace. We see the bigger picture. Believe in us not to give you the answer that you may want, but the answer that it most true.

We are a team- you and us. Our differences complement each other. We see the view; you move the energy. Together we extend the creation of human life.

YOUR FOREVER TIME

We will talk about the beginning and the end of time. The time as you know it to be. You know of time as a beginning and an end. The hour began, the hour ended. A new hour began and ended. Within your time, a job was started and a job ended. And so it goes with the beginning of time in linear form. Linear form exists in your world, in your mind. It isn't an absolute. Outside of your mind- in your spirit self, and your connection to oneness self, is infinite time. It doesn't begin or end. It never will. You see, infinite time is where you live. Therefore you always will-live. Your form will change yet you are timeless. Now would be a good time to make the best of your "always."

Start by realizing that your best is what makes you happy. Isn't that simple? Isn't that good to know? In endless time, you, in one form or another will be creating. Always have, always will. Your creation helps to feed endless forever. The energy you create- shall we say, lasts a long time. The energy you create will reverberate through all of time. Powerful you! All of those swirls of energy in foreverland were created by life forms. To know foreverland, look into outer space. View the cosmos. View the contributions from life forces over thousands of years. Spectacular wouldn't you say. You, the creator of a happy foreverland- that's a fantastic reality of your never ending time

THE CHANGES ARE BEING CREATED

It is an excellent time to write about the coming of peace. It is coming whether or not YOU realize this, and whether or not YOU put positive energy into the process. You see, there is energy of positive growth which has begun to circulate. Many people are promoting this positive energy, and these people are creating the changes necessary to save Earth. In time, everyone will join in. This message is simply an awareness. It doesn't mean that YOU need to wake up to the new energy today, or become enlightened today, or believe today. This is only a message of awareness. We are asking that you only "hear" the message today. In your good time, you will believe. Meanwhile, begin looking around for signs. The signs will present themselves to you in ways of change. Begin looking at the changes which are already occurring. The changes may not appear to be peaceful- they may appear to be chaotic. Look deeper. On the surface the chaos looks like struggle with opposing views. Look deeper. Can you see the opposition being due to change? Can you see that what was once acceptable is now challenged? Many forms of separation have been overlooked. Now it is coming to light. Separation with religions, politics, human rights, animal rights... It is coming to light that all life is about love. Accept the changes. Everyone is valued equally; everyone creates positive or negative energy. What are you creating today? Look deeper. Look at what you are creating. See the changes that are coming in you, and in the world.

NO MORE FIGHT FOR SURVIVAL

The time has come to discuss the view of a new Earth. The view is spectacular from our perspective. Visualize world peace. There has been enough talk about it over the centuries. Now it is becoming a reality. People of Earth are finally in the position to create from a caring and loving place. People of Earth can now think more logically, and see the bigger picture. The picture is not about self-centered greed, power, fear, anger. The picture is about living together peacefully, respectfully, and lovingly. It is coming. The times are changing. In the past, life fought for survival. In the future, life will love for survival.

VIEWING YOUR POWER OF CREATION

Let's talk about the view. What do you want to see, to hear, or to be? Do you look for the good news or the bad news? Do you create your own good and bad from neutral experiences? It is time to take a closer look at your creation of energy. You have the power, and the responsibility to create the energy of life. As we have said, the energy of life is love. Love, joy, happiness, creates and continues life. Love/life feeds the existence of all that is. Infinite everything is fed with love. This is good for you to know. This is your purpose while being in physical body. We invite you to take responsibility for your being. Take responsibility by seeing the goodness. This isn't merely a suggestion, or an overused phrase; it is your job. It is your gift to all that is. We want you to create for the goodness of all.

Some people on Earth talk about "The Creator" as if it were a man/god in a faraway place and time. We are telling you that YOU are the creator. The energy is everywhere. You are the manipulator of energy. Energy is the substance of all that is. Energy is the smallest denominator of everything. This is where your power is best used. The power of positive energy is life sustaining. I hope we are making it clear that your love, your joy, your happiness is good for you and for all that is. The more positive energy you create, the more you receive. If you feel negative energy in your life, in your world, in your situation, change it. You have the power and the responsibility. View the good stuff. Look for the good stuff. It is all around you. Good stuff is in that person you don't like, the situation you don't like, and even in yourself whom you don't always like. Focus on the better stuff. See that part of yourself and your world. See the view of your choice.

Now many of you will begin to argue with these words. You will begin to say that there is no "goodness" in that person, or situation. We say to take responsibility by adding goodness to that person or situation. Find the goodness either within you are them then share it. Find the love within yourself, and then share it. Create from your place of love. Is that clear, is that understandable? We think you are beginning to understand your power.

We recognize that there is the time and the place for acceptance. Overall, now is a good time and a good place to accept your position of power. While you are in physical form and on physical earth, accept your power and your ability to create and move the highest energy frequency of life. The energy frequency of love is the most powerful frequency that you can partner up with. Now is a perfect time to accept this power and to use it for the better good of you and all that is.

IMAGINATION

Now we will talk about The Time Will Tell. It is understood that time is the holder of all information. Every question and every answer is recorded in time both past, present, and future. Of course in our knowledge there is no past or future. There is wherever you want to be at any time. Your world is a part of a timeless whole. We are saying this so that you might imagine a larger picture; the larger picture of creation. Imagination is important because it will help to get you from here to there. Imagination is a key which will unlock many truths, and imagination will take you many places in infinite time. For now we would like for you to travel in your imagination to a place of discovery. Truly relax into

imagination that is beyond your present self and place. As you do, become aware of your weightlessness. Open your mind, your thoughts to the expansion of your infinite self. Probably what you see will be echoes of another time. Probably you will see yourself experiencing a larger picture. Our suggestion is that you relax and breathe into this larger picture. If it is in your mind, your imagination, it is in your reality.

Now, the point of this experiment is to introduce you to time travel. With time travel, you can experience all that you can imagine. It is real because it is energy, and all energy is real. We invite you to learn- to accept this part of realness. You see, all the modern conveniences would not be here without the reality of time travel with imagination. The more you practice, the more real it will become.

This is growth, this is expansion. This is becoming more than your physical self. Instead of black and white, two dimensional views, opening to imagination is opening to multi facets of possibilities. We invite you to live large. Use your imagination and soar into inexperienced realms. Get comfortable, allow your mind to leave your current awareness, and soar into the unknown. Imagine peace, be in peace, experience peace. Know your possibilities.

HOW TO THINK WITH AWARENESS

Let's talk about construction of thoughts and ideas. We are quite sure everyone has a time and place to think and create. Now may be a good time to consider the thoughts being created. Awareness is usually a good idea when creating. Awareness will get you to your desire a lot quicker, more directly, and more simply. Awareness means to create purposefully. Oh you might eventually get to the same place without awareness but it will take longer and can be more stressful.

We will explain the process of awareness on an energy circuit. Let's say it is prosperity that you want. You're thoughts become *I want* [prosperity]. The energy circuit picks up this message as *I want instead of I have*. Do you desire wanting or do you desire having. Do you see yourself wanting for the next few years or having for the next few years? The energy will return to you the energy that you sent out. You are the power, the driver. The energy is the response. Happiness, love, joy, etc. are energies. So is sadness, depression, longing. We continue to say, choose the highest frequencies. Have awareness of the frequencies you are using. That is the message. Let me repeat, Have Awareness of the Frequencies You Are Using. The more often you live in high energy frequencies (HEF) the more often your awareness is in the right place to receive that which you desire.

Now probably, you desire more than financial prosperity. You probably desire all the joy that comes with abundance. Focus on the joy, the love, the happiness that you want. By doing so, you will be taking the most direct path. You will be eliminating a lot of the time consuming drama. Focus on what you want, and then surround it with HEF as if your desire already exists- which it does. The more HEF in your life, the less desire you will have. Your awareness will be aligned with *I have* instead of *I want*. High energy frequencies of love, joy, happiness are the most direct path to anything you want. Become that which you seek.

THE LARGER VIEW OF YOU

We are here to say that you are love and you are loved. And now let's talk about the scope of the larger view. We say larger view because each of you has a physically limiting view because of your limited exposure to all that is. Another way to say this is that you can only be what you have experienced. We also consider thoughts and dreams as being a part of your experiences. This statement is not a judgment, just recognition that everyone's world view is based on their experiences. It can be no other way- unless you tune in to your spiritual self. Once again, when we say spiritual self we are not talking about a religious self, or a be-what-others-say-I-should-be self. We are talking about a true and real connection to your deeper self; the self that is connected to all that is. Now, that is the bigger part of you, and the part with many more experiences. It is the part that some people don't even believe exists. Your spiritual connection to all is your view, your advantage point to all that is. For all of you who are interested, we offer guidance so that you can view the wholeness of all. It's magnificent, spectacular, amazing and fulfilling.

Follow our lead to the greater part of your existence. It starts with belief. You can't get on track until you believe that there is something larger than your experiences- your physical existence- your brain. Next is willingness. If you believe in the possibility of a larger view, but are unwilling to look for it, to journey towards it, then you won't see it. Your journey is moved forward with desire to experience a greater part of you and the whole of all that is. Once you have belief, willingness, and desire, opportunities will become available to you. Opportunities which were always available, but which now you seek, will become noticeable. Understand that the path is open, only when you allow it to be. Understand that you are the person with the lever to switch paths. Once you do, the signs will appear. Not just in your "brain" but also in your spirit, or your intuitiveness. Know that you are on the path of your desire when you feel the goodness, when you like what you are reading, hearing, learning, experiencing. Know that you are on the right path when you enjoy, when your spirit, feels joy. The path can last a life time. Start at any time from any place. Now is a good time and a good place to begin experiencing a larger you.

THE TEACHERS OF NOW

We, the teachers, are a group of energy forms combined to send messages of peace. It is our mission to have the messages delivered of love, peace, joy, etc. Many energy forms (spirits) are available to help deliver the messages. We are known as the Jeshua group. You can also think of us as the Jesus group although we are more than Jesus. We are separate energy forms with a common cause. Each of us contributes to the messages in the NOW books. Each of us speak with our own voice, our own energy, yet we also speak as a group. If you read the word "I" or "We" know that I am talking for us. We all agree on the messages. In time, there may be separate books by a single teacher. For NOW, the books are a contribution from several sources, several Teachers. All of us teachers have walked in physical form on planet Earth. Some of us by name you would recognize, others slipped silently in and out of physical form. We have been a part of many countries, many time periods, and have represented many views. While in body, we all spoke of peace and love, and we continue to do so now.

For all the questions about how, and why to live in physical body on Earth, we are giving you the answers. For all the suffering you experience we are offering you a way out; a way into peace. In your own time, begin your journey of understanding. The end of the journey is a peaceful existence. You can start with doubt, and end with acceptance. You can start with anger and end with love. You see, it doesn't matter where you start. All roads lead to peace. We suggest you begin NOW. The Books of Now are about beginning NOW. Do you get it? Do you understand that we have walked in your shoes? We understand your concerns. We have the answers NOW. Join us whenever you are ready. We are all one with the energy of love.

THE VIEW FROM ONENESS

We will talk about becoming one. The time has come for understanding of everyone's connection. There seems to be an absence of belief or knowledge of oneness in some people. We will talk of how we are all connected. There is an energy that is invisible to most people. This energy won't always be invisible. With technological advancements- and with advancement in personal willingness, the energy will be seen. The same is true for now being able to see bacteria, sperm, and other small existing things. Anyway, there is an energy which is a part of everyone. This energy flows through all of what is, and further than you can imagine. ALL is a part of this energy. No thing, and no one can be excluded. This energy is your connection to all that is. Therefore, all people (and things) are connected to each other through the energy of life. You call it infinite love. By any name, no one is excluded from this connection. Now, people on Earth often act as if some are better, richer, or more powerful while others are poor, weak, etc. Let me say again that you are all connected to the same force with an equally powerful connection. In the most basic denominator, everyone is equal. The physical form that you have taken differentiates one from anther. The physical form is a placeholder necessary for creating change. No more, no less. In the picture of all that is, all physical forms are valued equally. It should bring you comfort to know that the bully, is just acting out a role. The bully is not more important. The same is true for the homeless. They are here in body to act out a role and bring awareness for the purpose of change. In a larger view, they are valued as are you. It would help a great deal if everyone would view the homeless, the bully, and all else, as awareness makers. Recognize the differences and respond from the connection that you all share. That connection is energy. That energy is HEF (the highest energy frequency). HEF is what you call love- infinite love. Once everyone begins to respond with HEF, the bullies will stop bulling, the homeless will have shelter, the hungry will have nourishment, the fearful will have love. Is this beginning to make sense?

We understand that in your role playing physical self, it is difficult to love the one who murdered your loved one and it is difficult to love the one who is littering your community with make-shift shelters. The sooner you begin to respond from your connection to them, your highest energy frequency, the sooner the problems will disappear. Respond from your connection to all, not from your temporary, separated, physical role. Practice responding with your larger view. Respond from your oneness, your connected self.

ALIGNING WITH UNCONDITIONAL LOVE

We are of course drawing from infinite energy. We speak to you with words from the energy of all that is. The energy of love is the energy of life. For now, let's call it the highest energy frequency.

As you in human form speak of love, it is conditional or limited. Your truth of love has been "if you..." then I will love you." When we speak of love, we speak of life, ultimate existence. We speak of an energy frequency. We don't have a name for it. We have a comprehension, a feeling, a knowing. You can too. It is available to everyone. Call it whatever you want but know that we are talking about the highest frequency, the longest vibration, the energy of life. You can experience this. When you experience unconditional love and joy, you are experiencing the greatest energy available. Open up. Accept what is yours. Let go of the limits, the boundaries, the walls. Experience freely, openly and lovingly. The energy of Earth will grow and continue to vibrate into forever. Each of you plays a role. Each of you participates in one way or another towards the energy of earth. It is our suggestion that you choose consciously. We suggest that you practice aligning with your inner truth which is unconditional, pure love.

CHANGING FOREVER

It is now time to concentrate on forever. You see, there is a time for everything. There is a time to forgive, to accept, to change and adjust. Now is the time for life on Earth to make this change. You are important to the coming changes. You are here to create the change- to move energy. We invite you to consider your purpose. The whole, total purpose of your life on earth, your being here is to create love. It is that simple. We see that some of you do not recognize your purpose. We also see that you often don't recognize this purpose in others. Recognition is coming. Eventually, everyone will "get it." For now, practice your own role while in physical form without judging the role of others. Each person has a job to do which will eventually bring peace and love to Earth. Don't question. Live your truth, your job. You might, however, want to occasionally step out of your limited view to see a bigger picture. Instead of judging, blaming, belittling etc., step back and know that each person has a role and each person is bringing awareness to others. Your role is to find your connection within. That means to find your connection to infinite love, to peace, to acceptance. Your role starts with *you*, not them. It's your time. You are in body to create change. Create the change that will last forever, create a loving environment.

SUSTAINING EARTH WITH YOUR GREATNESS

Now we are interested in telling you about the final result. It brings us great pleasure to assure you that there is enough positive energy to sustain life on Earth. We are pleased to announce that the energy of Earth will be changing towards the positive. You will participate. *YOU* will understand that the greatest good will be contributed from your greatness. Your greatest power is love and everyone will participate in the contribution of love to the energy of Earth. You can continue now, you can start now, or you can start in another life time. But you will participate. Your soul, your spirit, your life is based in love, and all of who you are will begin shining with your infinite love. There can be no other way. You cannot be separated from your substance and your substance is love. Become clear with this information. The sooner you recognize your role, the sooner you begin to participate. Recognize that love = life. Become the force that you are. It is with love that we share these words. It is with love that you will fulfill your purpose. Prepare and go forth with love.

And now we will talk about the coming of the new times. It is with joy that we continue to remind you of your strength. Each and every one of you has the strength and the power of greatness because you are each connected to the infinite whole of all-that-is. We suggest that you become comfortable with using your power. For the greater good of you, your community, and your planet, tune within to your infinite love.

It is time to consider your greatness. Because you are oneness with all, you *are* all. You are a part of all the greatness that exists. Just like a raindrop is a recycled part of the ocean, you are a recycled part of infinite all. Your body will recycle through earth; your spirit will recycle through all of time. Get to know your strength, your power. Become comfortable with the all of you. The all-of-you is so much more than the problem you have. As a matter of fact, the all-of-you doesn't have a problem or a need. If you will begin accepting that part of you, the physical problems will begin to diminish. When you begin to live from love, problems begin to vapor away. Try it for a while. Become comfortable with all-of-you. By doing so, you will become comfortable with all of them. And that is your purpose.

ADJUSTING TO CHANGE

We will talk now about the coming firestorms. What we mean to say, the disruptions that will happen on Earth. It is clearly time for awareness of the changes your planet will experience. As the energy of earth changes, so will events. Some things will have to crash before rebuilding can happen. This is all how it should be. Sometimes an old building is torn down before the new building can be erected. In this case, old beliefs have to come down so that new beliefs will emerge. With the changing of beliefs will be a change in actions. The change in actions will create a new system with a foundation in peace. Your laws, religions, financial institutes, prisons, educational systems... will change. Allow the restructuring. Look beyond the appearance of what is before you; beyond the destruction. Instead, look forward with a vision of coming peace. You are living in a time of transition. Accept change. The best way of doing this is to be open. That really means to open your heart, your thoughts, and your beliefs. That is all you need to do. Allow yourself the freedom to explore. Allow.

The time is now to let go of your "secure" vision of how you view the world. The time is now to look beyond your limited view. Consider that there is a view much larger than yours. Consider that we have seen *all* the struggles through time. Consider that we have seen developing beliefs and we have seen the death of many beliefs and institutions. We see that what survive are the beliefs in love for all. Believe in the whole of all that is. Believe in love for all.

BE THE VIEW OF PEACE

There is a time to overlook and a time to see clearly the view directly in front. Now is that time. NOW is the time to view a peaceful world. If you can't see it or imagine it then you will have a difficult time constructing it. We recognize that you want peace- in yourself, your community, your planet. We also recognize that the peace will come from you. All the "yous" in the world will have to construct peace. Don't expect others to construct for you. Let others set examples of peace. Then follow their examples or create your own for others to follow. Look for examples of peace. Overlook the negative in what you read- look for the peaceful words. If you don't see them, create your own peaceful words to share with others. Listen for the peaceful sounds. If you don't hear them, create your own peaceful sounds or music then share it with others. What we are saying is that it is your turn to create peace. Become a leader in the revolution of peace. Everyone can become a leader. Everyone has the potential; what is needed is desire. Desire peace, visualize peace, and create peace. Be the view of peace that others will see. We see you.

What do you expect? What do you want? What are you doing to get it? Are you interested in being at peace? If so, then know that peace is yours to create. Become aware of your attitudes, your thoughts, and your beliefs. The mountain you will be moving is inside of you. Your journey begins internally not externally. Don't be looking out there or at "them." YOUR peace will come from within whenever you choose to monitor your attitudes, thoughts, and beliefs.

AT THE CELEBRATION

We can share with you a view of a peaceful world. Imagine an event where everyone is happy, joyful, feeling love. Maybe it is a celebration where many have gathered. Imagine the "plentiful-ness" of fine food and refreshments. Imagine that everyone is feeling equally important and pleased to be at this celebration. Can you get an overall feeling of this picture? We hope so. Hold the imagination a bit longer and expand it to cover the entire planet. Imagine that everyone on planet Earth is enjoying this celebration. We could call it a Happy Earth Day celebration. Now imagine that overall, this is an everyday energy of planet Earth. Oh there might be little dramas here and there, but they don't last long. Mostly everyone is joyful. Even when their loved ones transcend out of physical body, there is celebration. There will be gratitude for all the food and drink- no one will be hungry or thirsty because everyone will live on a planet of plentiful-ness. Crime and punishment are events of the past. Imagine that sickness has decreased dramatically. It is possible. This view of future Earth is real and made possible by changing negative energy into positive energy. Each person is a change maker. Your job while in physical form is to create and expand positive energy. While in physical form, you can move the mountain. Move to the positive, away from the negative. At your celebration release your drama, embrace your joy. Do the same for Earth. It is time. In advance of your future cooperation, we thank you.

EARTH'S UPGRADE IS GOING ON

It is now time to discuss the goings-on with Earth. Your planet, your home, your responsibility. It is time to talk about the upgrade to a planet with higher frequency. It is Earth's time to upgrade. You are the controller- the button pusher. Earth will upgrade when its energy systems upgrade. The people of Earth are the networking systems responsible for creating the peaceful planet. If you could see and experience the future peaceful planet, we think you would be more eager to create the upgrade. You see the future peaceful planet will be a lot more stress free. We think you want a more stress free way of being. Start now. Each day there is time in your schedule to be grateful. Gratitude is a stress free state of being. Each day there is time and reason to smile and experience moments of joy. Become conscious of these moments. Expand them. Be the button pusher for the higher frequencies which will sustain life on Earth. It is your job, your responsibility, and you have the power. We think your job is a fun one. Your responsibility is to notice and improve on your joy, your love, your happiness, your smiles. Doing so is a part of the goings-on with Earth. Participate regularly.

COLOR CODES

Looking in from out here, we see your energy. That is to say we see the energy of Earth. As we said before, you have energies and so does your planet. For that matter, all of life- and all *is* life- has energy. It is a spectacular view. In your media photos of Earth, you're mostly aware of a white aura. With advance technology, your earth pictures will be able to show the other colors surrounding your planet. It is OK to think of the color as coding for health. See the colors- the energy frequency- and you can see the health. The lighter, brighter your color of Earth, the better the health. The same is true for you. Your aura says a lot about what you are experiencing and radiating into forever. We suggest that you learn to see the colors. There are people who can see auras, and there is equipment that can see colors. Use them and develop them. Do so not as a judgment but as a helpful guide towards peace. Technology has developed instruments for seeing color, other instruments are a part of everyone. Some persons have been able to tune in to this part of them. Yes, there are millions of people who can see auras. Mostly these people have learned not to speak of this ability, therefore letting their color detection decline. Such a waste. It would be much more beneficial to use the ability to see these color codes to help others and the planet. We encourage everyone to look in from out there. No matter how you see the colors of energy we suggest that you continue to see that all is alive. And so it shall be.

DISCOVERING THE TRUTHS ABOUT GOD

We will talk about discovering the truths of your existence. We see a lot of search for the answers to life on Earth and how to make the best of life. We can tell you that most answers you seek are in plain sight. What you seek is confirmation of existence. The truths will be revealed with discovery. That is to say that the answers have always been here. Nothing is hidden or left out. All of Earth, life, the cosmos, is one truth. Actually, your life and the life of earth are a part of the greater picture of the cosmos, the universe, the all that is. The *all* is far greater than you can imagine. Try to imagine forever without end. Such is the space which surrounds your planet. Eventually, with discovery, this truth will become a known instead of a thought or an idea. Eventually inhabitants of earth will discover that they are a part of a never ending forever. If you want to look for a beginning, look at love. Once again, we don't mean physical or limited love- we mean infinite love. Once again we say "love" is an insufficient human word. The word itself cannot capture the essence or the strength of an infinite life force. Some of you call it God. It isn't a god. It is an energy.

We tell you this to express the greatness of all that is. You have a role in this greatness. The energy that you call infinite love can also be called infinite life. It feeds upon itself. The energy of infinite life is a high frequency. Let us say again that space, as you call it, is infinite which goes much further than imagination. You are and always will be a part of all- the energy of life/love.

It is time to discover that God- all of your different versions of God, are man-made explanations of the greatness of life. In simple terms, life- is love- is energy. It is not a man-made story which brings separation and suffering. Actually, it is the opposite. The separation and restrictions of religions and gods creates suffering which creates opposition to expansion and life. Oh, don't think there is enough power in separation to end infinity. Separation is a waste of time. What people of Earth will be discovering is that being a part of infinite all, the energy of infinite love is your truth and your answer. The energy of infinite love is a part of you, and it is your connection. You connect through high frequencies. High frequencies begin with love and travel through joy, happiness, giggles, and grins. By experiencing high energy frequencies, (HEF) you will be experiencing and maintaining the flow, the movement of infinite space.

We invite you to continue the discovery. We invite you to enjoy your time on Earth. Experience the wonderful discovery of truths. In time, everyone will understand. Your time begins when you are ready to discover the truths of love and life.

THE BOOKS OF LOVE- RELIGION

Religions are beliefs but not necessarily truths. We understand how religions create a sense of conformity, structure, and a belief system which is shared by a group. This creates a sense of individual stability and purpose along with a sense of belonging and of community. The same can be said with many forms of "joining." Our suggestion is that you consider joining for the purpose of creating peace for all of Earth. Is your religion exclusive or inclusive of everyone? Probably your first thought would be that your group is open to everyone. Are *you* open to everyone? Does *your* personal belief, the one which is shared by your personal religion, include a love for all life on earth? We invite you to discover a deeper awareness. Look deeper within. Not within the rules or guidelines of your religion, but within yourself and your beliefs. Does your love cross all boundaries, all separations, and all differences? Is there any other "group" or belief that is in conflict with your group or belief? It may be time to expand your view and beliefs. We tell you that it *is* time for expansion and inclusion.

Every person on planet earth is a member of a much larger group. This larger group holds the interest of every single person as well as every life form. Whether or not you know it, you as well as everyone else, are a member of the greatest truth, the greatest love, and the greatest life form. Now is a good time to learn the rules and guidelines so that you can practice a new set of beliefs.

These new practices and beliefs are about an inclusion of love for every life form. If you need a new book to read and practice from, we are providing it. We are providing the books of love. Our words resonate within everyone. No one is excluded because in the spirit, the soul, the heart of every person is infinite love. All anyone needs to do is connect from this place. In our books, there is no judgment, no separation, or no good versus evil. Our books are about love for everyone. Is your book about love for all? Is your belief about love for all? Is it time for expansion? We are ready to help you expand into a love that reaches every planet, every galaxy, and every universe.

Our suggestion is that you adopt the books of love; the belief in everyone and all of life. We are here to help you- and always have been. We, THE TEACHERS OF LOVE.

HORIZONS

There comes a time to look beyond your horizon; that which you cannot see yet exists. Now is a good time. Imagination is often a good place to start. Imagination will shake up some of the old ways of thinking and old belief systems. What do you imagine is visible on the other side of the horizon? More earth? More water, land, flora and fauna- more people? Realize that this is your imagination brought on by past experiences. There is more than you can see or imagine. There is a forever that you are a part of and that you are feeding in to. You are in a time of knowing. This is an evolutional time of becoming a whole and complete person in physical form as well as a person who is guided by their spiritual self. It can also be known as a time of awakening to greater self. Yes, we like that. An awakening to your greater self is happening. Instead of your limited physical world self, which can be quite painful, humans are awakening to the whole of who they are. The whole of everyone is the physical and the spiritual. Wake up! Enjoy the more peaceful loving part of you. Enjoy life from the perspective of love. You can. It is available, and desirable. Practice.

Live as if you know there is something greater past the horizon of your physical existence. When you know it, and live by it, many of your dramas will end. The dramas just won't be as significant. The more dramas you let go of, the more peaceful will be your existence. Isn't that your desire? Peace. With peace comes joy and love. We are here to help. Begin by knowing that everywhere you go, love, peace, and joy exist. Allow the awakening. See past your physical horizon into your infinite loving self.

RELEASE AND REALIGN

There comes a time for everyone to realize their greater selves. This is a good time. You see, the fussing in your physical life can be eliminated if you choose. We say this to remind you that the best of life is always available- if you choose. In order to have the best, let go of the worse. Doesn't that sound simple? Yes, it is simple but will take practice. Most people practice rolling around in the negative energy. Oh they don't do it as a conscious choice, they usually do it with a bit of blame, judgment, and some "woe-is-me." We are telling you that you have a choice as to the type of energy you choose to roll around in. At any time, in any place, any scenario you can let go of negative energy and become aligned with positive energy. In your worst scenario you can surrender its negative energy. Surrender. Let it go, give up, give in. Those awful worries can disappear as quickly as they arrived- if you choose. The choice is to surrender the worries, the bad temper, the blaming, the criticism... When you do, you'll probably experience a physical difference. Shoulders will drop, a breath will release, headache will disappear, body tensions will release- once you let go and surrender your response. Allow. Allow negative energy to leave you so that positive energy can fill you. With the positive energy will be answers on the energy waves of peace, love, joy. Practice releasing. Make it a new life style- a new pattern of being. Align with love, peace, and joy. Make it a habit. Perceived negative events will still come your way. They just won't be *in* your way.

OPTIONS FOR MAKING IT HAPPEN

It is time for discovery of new options. You see, People of Earth are largely stuck in negative behavior thoughts, and beliefs. Old habits and old ways of being have become the comfortable yet dissatisfying norm. Conscious awareness will create change.

44

These books and these teachings are meant to create awareness. We suggest that you all become aware of the different types of energy and the energy that you are most commonly using. In simple words, that means how often do you smile versus how often do you frown. We are familiar with all the reasons, excuses, and conditions that you have. We are also familiar with your choices for making the best, most rewarding life for all of Earth and beyond. Your happiness is your strength, you unhappiness is your weakness. *None* of your strengths or weaknesses are because of your experiences. NONE! Choosing to live in positive strength or negative weakness is always your choice. I understand that bad things happen and that you may be the victim or perpetrator of bad things because of something that was done to you. Still, it is your choice- allow your pain and suffering to continue or let it go and allow love to continue. If you don't know how, start there. Start by saying "I don't know how." You are now on the path. From your heart, your center, your connection, (not your brain) acknowledge your position and then acknowledge your desire. Are you pleased with what you have had, currently have, will have? If you can find pleasure, now would be a good time to express gratitude. If you are currently starving but at some time have had a full belly, give thanks for that time. If in the future you want an abundance of good nutrition, give thanks for the time you had, and the time you expect to receive more. Give thanks in advance of the receiving. If there have been spoonfuls of food that have kept you alive, give thanks. At some time, after practicing, you will actually be able to *feel* the joy and gratitude. You will become a believer in acknowledging all you have consumed. It is at that time, when you believe, you recognize, and you give thanks, that more of what you desire will be showered upon you. It is at this time that your energy will shift from negative to positive. The good stuff comes through positive energy. Make it happen.

VIEW THE KINDNESS OF NEW EARTH

There is a new world, a new experience coming. Same Earth, different energy. The transition has begun. For those of you who are ready, now is the time to view a different existence. In time everyone will be able to live in positive energy. For now, some have discovered the path, others will, within the time of their readiness. We say this so as to bring awareness of change. You all have the ability to create this change to a loving peaceful Earth. It is the *yous* in physical form who will create a new experience. Now is the time to view a peaceful forever on Earth. View it, imagine it, create it, become peace. Practice. Let the thoughts and beliefs of peace begin to resonate within you. Begin seeing others as equals with you. In your own way, recognize the goodness in others. Once you recognize the goodness in others, talk about it. Share a story of goodness that came from someone. Make it a habit. Let go of old story telling regarding your dislike in another. Now is the time to create new experiences of kindness. Imagine the results. View future earth by visualizing kindness.

YOUR ANSWERS ARE IN LOVE

Good day. Another good day to write about the love of all. Through all your worries and all your grief, we wish for you to hold on to love- the best energy available. For any cure or any solution finder, love is always an answer. If you are trying to figure out a major problem, love is still a way. You see, the energy of love is the energy of life and the energy of eternity. All the answers are within love. That is because we see love as more than a great feeling in the heart or a good connection to another. Love is also another word for god, the whole, source.... The answer to all is love. But of course that may not mean a lot to everyone. Yet it is the answer. I can assure you that all your answers will come from love. That is a fact. All your answers for all your questions will come from love. Oh yes, you can create a multitude of non-truthful, non-factual answers; those which come from your limited brain. The brain answers are good for serving your limited physical existence. I don't mean to dismiss your limited physical existence which is important yet, I mean to say that the answers you seek will be found in love=life.

YOUR JOB WHILE HERE ON EARTH

We are happy for you. Let's begin. Now is the time to talk about forever. Want to take a peek? Forever is on an energy level. It is not visible with your eyes- yet it exists for every person, place, thing, animal, plant... Got the picture of importance? You see, forever is eternal- you are a part of forever so that makes you eternal. Of course your physical form will recycle throughout time. It is the energy of your loving self, your spiritual self that lasts forever. This brings us to the point- while here on Earth, live lovingly. Make it easy on yourself, everyone around you, and the universe. Live as if... hmm, as if grins, laughter, hugs, kisses, loves, forgiveness, helpfulness, and happiness is your reason for being here. Live in high energy frequencies because that is the job of your physical self. You are here to create and expand high energy frequency (HEF). Know your purpose. Practice your purpose often. Live your purpose. Your spirit can not do this without a body.

We know that the body has limited time on Earth. We suggest you use your physical body to live more peacefully. The best way to accomplish this is to live with less greed, judgment, hatred, blame, sadness, or hurtfulness. Even when times get rough, keep tuning into your loving self. Stay as long as you can in your loving self. Stay with the part of you who *feels* from the love within. Practice.

THE REALITY OF INFINITE SPIRIT

It is time to experience a different reality. If your reality is peaceful, mostly calm, without drama, with bursts of happiness and smiles, chances are you live from your infinite spiritual self. If your reality is often negative then it may be time to change, YES, YOU HAVE A CHOICE. And yes the choice and the change are easily achieved. This is where we hear people begin to focus on all the "buts." But if only this or that would change. You are the change maker; the events in your life are not. You have the power not the events.

We recommend that you start with acknowledging. Take some time to notice. Just notice. When you are alone, are you usually in positive energy or in negative energy. When you are with others, are you usually in positive or negative energy? Notice and become aware of your energy. It is that simple.

Next, be quiet. Sit quietly release, let go. Give it up, surrender. Tears may come with this part. Let them go too. Shhhh. Your brain may kick in at this time- thinking it will save you. Don't listen. Simply let go. Shhh. Breathe and let go.

Tune in to your inner spirit connection. The place you sometimes call "heart." Feel the energy. The energy of life is for everyone in forever time. Not only for those in current physical body. While you are there, give gratitude, feel gratitude.

Repeat regularly.

A GOOD THING ABOUT FOREVERLAND

We are so very pleased to have you back with us. We will talk more about forever. The reason is that you all live in foreverland so you might want to get used to it. Once you can accept a place of forever, then your attitudes, beliefs, and choices will probably change. You see, if you live as if your spirit has all the time in the world- which it does, then you might live more peacefully and more purposefully.

Once your body and spirit separate, the body will of course recycle back to Earth. Your spirit however, will live on in forever time. At any time, your spirit will have the choice of reentering the physical realm in another body for a different experience. All experiences are, in one way or another, related to the positive expansion of energy. Those living in negative energy are still moving towards positive energy. Try not to judge them. Eventually everyone will be living in positive energy. It just takes time to evolve as a planet. But as we have said, all spirits have plenty of time to evolve and live peaceful, happy, loving lives. No matter where you are on the peaceful evolution cycle, try not to judge others who may be on a different cycle. Eventually all paths will join as one peaceful planet. That is one good reason to be thankful for foreverland.

THE CHANGING TIMES

Time to talk again about the View From Now. When you (or we) view the 10th century recorded in books or documentaries, the view is a lot different than the view of the 17th century. So is the view of the current century different, and so will be the view of a future century. That is all easy to understand. It is fairly easy to see the changes in attitudes, perceptions, and knowledge. What we want to make clear is that it is the people of the times who make the changes. This is your time. You are making changes. What are you creating?

We think that is a good awareness question. We think it is good to live with awareness of your creations. In your attitudes, are you creating peace or war, fear or love? In your jobs, are you contributing within your ability to the betterment of all or the decline of all? These are also good questions to ponder. The answers will be in your inner truth. We aren't asking for perfection. We are simply asking for awareness. That is all; just awareness of your contributions to the changing times.

If you follow the thread of peace, love, joy in societies throughout time, we think you can see change. Look for the changes. Look for your contributions. Have a clear focus of what you would like future Earth to look like. Are you moving in that direction? Remember, every single person is a contributor. Millions of sand granules form a desert. Millions of snowflakes form a glacier. Millions of embodied spirits create a peaceful Earth. Every large and small contribution creates change. The energy which you exude is changing this century. We applaud you. Keep it up!

THE NEW AGE OF PEACE ON EARTH

It is time to write about the coming new age. The New Age of Peace. The planet Earth has evolved to the next level. It is a good time to celebrate the dawning of peace on earth. We understand that many of you don't see or experience the peace. We understand that most news stories are about conflict. We understand that all is not peaceful. We are simply stating that peace is more dominant, fear is more recessive. If the world had good news programs, there would be more peace to talk about than violence. We suggest that you start talking. Start talking about the peace in your world, your country and your community. Peace starts from within. When you recognize the peace inside of yourself, talk about it. From that peaceful place within, view peace in your area. Look for the smiles, the hand holding, and the playfulness. It's there. The more you see, the more you will become like a magnet to peace. We invite you to purposefully, with awareness, draw peace to you, your community and your planet. Align with the new age of peace on Earth.

EARTH CHANGERS

Want to see an awesome view? Try focusing on a planet in peace. As we have said, peaceful planets do exist and Earth will also be in peace. It will happen. The chaos will evolve into peace. All the awareness of differences will melt into loving acceptance. It isn't that difficult to imagine. Thought and imagination is where peace begins. Imagine peace. What do you see? Keep imagining, keep visualizing. As you do, peace is forming a reality because you are creating. Eventually, after enough people visualize, Earth will change. This is a simple truth. Each person must do their part. Many people are already practicing peaceful thoughts. Join them. Become one of the Earth changers. Merge with others who are changing Earth. All you need to do is view peace instead of viewing violence. Read about peace, talk about peace, become peace.

Can you visualize the people with hate and fear finding acceptance and joy? It is possible, and it will happen to everyone in their own time, in this life time or another. For those of you already experiencing peace, continue to light the way for others. That means, continue to smile, to love, to express joy and happiness. Continue tuning into your love within. The vision is alive. The view is spectacular.

ALIGN AND TALK ABOUT THE NEW AGE OF PEACE ON EARTH

It is time to write more about the coming new age of peace. The planet Earth has evolved to the next level. It is a good time to celebrate the dawning of peace on earth. We understand that many of you don't see or experience the peace. We understand that most news stories are about conflict. We understand that all is not peaceful. We are simply stating that peace is more dominant, fear is more recessive. If the world had more good news productions, there would be more peace than violence to talk about. We suggest that you start talking. Start talking about the peace in your world, your country and your community. Peace starts from within. When you recognize the peace inside of yourself, talk about it. From that peaceful place within, view peace in your area. Look for the smiles, the hand holding, and the playfulness. It's there. The more you see, the more you will become like a magnet to peace. We invite you to purposefully, with awareness, draw peace to you, your community and your planet. Align with the new age of peace on Earth.

YOUR ENERGY, YOUR CIRCUMSTANCES, YOUR CHOICE

Let's consider the comings and goings of energy. They are multi layered, co-existing, intertwining and aligning with each other. There is an abundance of energies for you to choose from. Mostly, out of habit, a comfort has developed with using a few energies. Mostly people don't recognize the choices. Mostly people get in a rut and live out life with a few basic energies while assuming there is no other choice. There seems to be a habit of blaming conditions for the surrounding energy. It is time to recognize that the energy you choose is the energy that will be drawn to you. Stop blaming the events, start choosing the energy you desire. Making choices starts with awareness. Become aware that you have the power to choose and your energy is not a victim of your circumstances. Your energy is your choice no matter what your circumstances may be. As you continue to choose the energy of your desire, your circumstances will align and more often become the circumstances of your desire. Let me clearly state that if you want peace, choose the energy of peace, live peacefully, recognize the peaceful circumstances that come to you, then speak in gratitude of what you created. The same goes for happiness, joy, sadness, loneliness.... Choose the energy, and watch it materialize. If you like what you created, express gratitude, if you don't like what you created, change the energy frequency. Once again, this simple formula requires awareness and practice. Keep it up!

BEGIN WITH YOUR OWN LIFE

Now, it is time to consider your options. While in this time of change and transformation, now is your time to join in. Consider that the choices you make will be affecting generations of life. Start with your own life. Let this be the time to breathe easier, to see the greatest, and to experience love and peace. Make it your goal, your vision to view success. In our view, success looks like happiness, peace, joy, and love. We hope it is your view also. Of course we are talking about spiritual success which goes along with physical success. There is no reason whatsoever to not have the earthly riches you desire. Start with a view. Can you see yourself as a spiritual entity in a physical body, on earth for the purpose of creating positive energy? Try. Even if for little bouts of joy, try knowing that you are here to produce positive energy. If you can achieve the view, practice living it and growing it. Share you joy with others so that they too experience happiness. There is no need to lecture, convince, preach, or judge. Just be in your own loving place. Others will notice the view from you. Some will respond others won't. It doesn't matter. Be your loving self and others will see your reflection. Allow all the richness to flow towards you. Bask in your joy then feel the greatness that comes to you. Watch for it, expect it, give thanks and gratitude. The option is yours.

LET'S MAKE AN AGREEMENT

It is with great love that we speak these words to you. It is our goal, our purpose to help the people of earth create an easier existence. If it is easier for the people, it will be easier for the animals, the plants, the planet, and into the infinite space. Go forth knowing that you are the creator of peace. You have the power- the power of love to create that which you desire. Desire peace, desire love, and desire joy. Know that this is the purpose of all people. Once everyone begins to understand and act from their place of love, everyone will also notice the abundance. Create with love, not fear. Your choice as always. Chose consciously.

We say this to help with the creation of a better view. You see, we hold a better view. We can see a greater planet. We can share our view for you to create. Let us share our view of a greater planet Earth. We will give you the picture, you create the reality. Deal?

Now, if you agree to create from a loving place, your infinite loving spiritual place, your physical existence will benefit. It can be no other way. We think that is what you want; a comfortable physical life. We think that everyone wants the basics of food, shelter, and love. Again we tell you that it is possible. There is enough of everything to comfort everyone. The deal is to include your spiritual self, your loving self.

YOUR MISSION FOR A LIFE SUPPORTING FUTURE

It is time to look beyond the present. Of course you will still see the present- and the past, but we also want you to view forward. From time to time, imagine Earth in a few hundred years from now. What do you imagine? If you imagined disease, famine, war, dead crops, then that is just what you may get. Now try again. Imagine a prosperous earth flourishing with abundance. Imagine clear and clean flowing water. Imagine life in full bloom. Can you see it? Keep trying. Now imagine people being kind to one another; caring for one another and sharing without fear. Be careful, if you can imagine it, then that is just what you may get.

That is the way it works. The seed starts in your imagination, your thoughts, your beliefs. Work within the flow. Stay out of the *way* yet join in the *way*. Join in the way of love and life. You are the way maker. Do you find that to be exciting? We do. We are excited to know that people on Earth will be creating the way of the future. On other planets, life forms created the way of their future. Join in with the creation. Know that you are important, valued, and loved.

What we are saying is to create with purpose. Understand your position in the whole of all that is. Develop awareness then act from that awareness. Whether you believe or disbelieve is not the issue. Act as if. Act as if your ability to create loving, live supporting energy is your purpose. It is.

HOW TO PROSPER FROM GIVING AND RECEIVING

Let's take some time to discuss the meaning of prosperity. When we use the word prosperity, we are speaking of abundance all around. We are including everyone, and we are not speaking of financial gain for a few. We are speaking of health all around, nutrition all around, and fun all around. All around includes all of Earth, all the plants, and animals. We are speaking of a prosperous ecosystem on Earth.

In order for all of Earth to prosper, sharing and receiving must happen. In order for sharing to happen, mind-sets and beliefs will need to change. Recognize that you all are givers and receivers. We suggest that you, on a personal level, practice the balance of giving and receiving. Do so with joy. Do so with awareness. Become aware of receiving, and then give gratitude from your heart; true gratitude, not just mumbled words. When giving, do so from your heart- with meaning. A rich and prosperous planet comes from giving and receiving from your place of love. The process is the same whether you are currently considered to be rich or poor. Shame, ego, judgment, or greed is not a part of this process. The feeling of lack and the feeling of entitlement are also not a part of the process. To achieve positive results, give and receive from your loving self. Everyone participates. Begin now with awareness. Feel the richness.

CONTEMPLATE YOUR POWER

Have you ever wondered about infinity? Have you ever contemplated forever? Right now, lean back, let go of your surroundings, and let your thoughts expand. Visualize the vastness of the great out-there. That greatness is a part of the great in-here. That is to say that all of what is, is an expansion of the same energy. All is made up of the same stuff. It is hard to imagine but try. The energy of everything is the energy of life. The pure, white, energy of life is the feeder of everything that is. This is a truth.

You are a creator of this energy of life. Each and every one of you creates the movement of energy. Your energy travels to the great out-there. As well, the energy of out-there travels to in-here. One flowing energy of forever. We hope you realize your importance. You see, it takes a physical mass to move this energy. The spirit world can't move energy. You are the energy expander of forever. We say this so that you may become aware of the energy you send out. It is the good stuff, the good energy that will keep Earth alive. It is within your power to manifest life on Earth for generations to come.

Contemplate your power. Take time to wonder about what you are creating. While doing so, realize that the energy you generate goes out there. Every smile, hug, laughter, and every frown, punch, or misdeed contributes to the energy of forever. You don't get a free pass or a day off. With every breath, you create.

56

Something to wonder about? Something to contemplate? Think about life; think about love, joy, and happiness. Act on it.

YOUR HERE, NOW, AND FOREVER LEGACY

Let's talk about the here and now. Let's talk about here, now, and forever. You see, right here, and right now, you are contributing to forever. Your results will show up here, now, and long after you are gone. That is why we ask you to become aware of your contributions. We ask that you re-think your legacy. What you leave for others can come from your heart, your spirit. Let it be a loving legacy. Let the positive energy which you create, become a part of all that is. Let the people who follow your transition (death) experience your loving, caring, joyful, and happy energy.

Right now, right here where you are is perfect for releasing positive energy. All you have to do is smile from your heart, laugh from deep inside, experience joy, or think happy thoughts. Right now, right here. Good. Now H.E.F (high energy frequencies) have been released for you and future generations to enjoy. We are pleased. Keep up the good work in the here, now, and forever.

YOUR DIRECTION TO INNER SELF

We are ready to discuss the course, the direction, the path to your other self; the self that is a part of you but that which you don't always recognize. This time pay closer attention. We will be specific. We are saying that you, ego, physical self, brain is only a part of the all of you. We think you understand by now yet perhaps you want to know the path for tuning in. Good. We hope you want to know. We also want you to know that every single answer to every single question is available to you- and might be different than what your brain wants to think. You can think of it as voodoo, cosmic intervention, magic, or whatever word you have for talking about the unknown. The truth is *LISTEN* without your ears. Feel the truth. Only you can open the channels of communication. We are always here; your spirit is always with you. Know in advance that you are being heard. All you need to do is let go of your programmed way of thinking through your brain. Surrender the brain, the thoughts and let go. The path is short, instant, and always available. All you have to do is practice the shhhs of the brain. Our words and spirit words will enter. Shhh. The words may sound like your thoughts or look like images. Practice awareness of the deeper part of you. Practice.

Perhaps the message is that "you have," yet you say "I have not." Or the message is of love but you say love lost. Recognize that we see further than your *now*. We see that you planted a seed. Relax, allow, and give it nurturing so it will grow. Nurture with your energy, and with gratitude. Let it be.

YOUR CREATIVE POWER OF H.E.F.

Let's be creative. It is time to create a different reality. The new reality is a part of your being but may not be a part of your conscious everyday thoughts. We want to help you bring the new reality into actualization. It *is* possible for everyone to adopt awareness of a higher way of being. Everyone has the potential to live in the light of positive energy. The energies of love, joy, happiness, and peace are a part of your makeup as are low energy frequencies. When you hear someone say, "I can't change the way I feel" maybe they don't want to change frequencies or maybe they are not aware of having the choice to change frequencies. We guarantee that everyone *can* change the way they feel. Everyone has the ability to create the frequency of choice.

We recognize the difficulty of changing frequencies by desire instead of as an automatic response to environmental conditions. Can you imagine the power you would have over daily situations if you could choose a frequency to respond with? It *is* an amazing power that you have. Practice awareness of choosing a frequency to respond with. Be aware that you don't have to respond consistently on automatic. It will take some time to correct the automatic process. It will take some time to learn manipulation of the frequencies. Expect to enjoy the different realities of your creativeness. Expect to enjoy your power of creating HEF (high energy frequencies)

PEACE IS YOUR RESPONSIBILITY

The time has come for recognizing responsibility. Gone are the days of living without awareness. Gone are the days of living without conscious awareness of what you are creating. You are all creating all of the time. Do so wisely, and make choices based on awareness. What we are saying is to stop living without purpose. Living without purpose creates more negative energy which is not conducive to life. Know that you are on Earth for a purpose and the purpose is to create positive energy which continues life for all and everything. Now, assume an understanding of peace for all. It is possible and within *your* power. Make way. Make the way for a peaceful planet. This is more than a dream; it is a reality as soon as you believe it to be. You are the creator and only you(s) can create the reality. For that matter it is the you(s) who created the reality thus far. All the love, joy, and happiness was created. All the prisons, murders, suicides were created. What you do for one affects all. The energy that you manifest expands to influence all of earth and beyond. Chose wisely and chose with the awareness of your power.

It is with great love that we approach you through these words. We are sending these words with purpose. We are hoping to guide the direction of energy towards peace. We can give direction but only you can chose to follow. The following comes not from us but from your inner wisdom, your inner knowledge of all that is. We are here to point you towards your inner strength, your inner power. Peace begins with you, not them or them or them. Now is a good time to be peaceful. Believe in your power, your strength, and your ability. Believe in peace.

AN EXPLANATION OF YOUR POWER

We are giving you these words for a reason, and the reason is to create conscious awareness of your personal strength for creating change. Take responsibility. It is your turn because you are the one on earth in physical life form, with the mass to create. When you were in spiritual form without a body, you understood the purpose and truth of life=love=life. In physical form, your spirit still believes. You are not guided solely by your brain. Wake up to a full awareness. You are not here to wander aimlessly or try to gather all of everything you can. Know that you are much more important to the larger picture. Learn to live together by first learning to love yourself. Love from your heart your infinite self. This love within will lead you to peace. Your energy of peace will expand. Your expanded energy of peace will create a loving expansion in others. You may not see it. You won't see it- yet it will happen. You will begin to feel the change within yourself. Others will be attracted by your change. Sometimes the attraction will be only for minutes. Other times the attraction will become life-long relationships. Your energy from your loving infinite self will continue to grow with or without your ability to see. That is where to begin- begin with loving your loving self. Does that help you to understand your power of creation?

THE CHANGING EARTH

Now we will tell you about the beginning of a new adventure for Earth. Because so many of you have become aware and are working on living in positive energy, life on Earth is changing. Some of you can see it, and some never will- yet we see the changing energy. Maybe you can *feel* the difference. Yes, we are sure that some of you can feel the difference while others still live in fear. That is the course for this stage of progress. Everyone is in line and everyone is participating in their rightful time. For those of you who recognize the difference show kindness to those who don't. It is through your kindness that they will see the light to follow. Recognize that all is advancing as it should.

Want to know about the changes being made? Those of you who have learned to experience self love have awakened to the method of change. We realize that awakening to self love is a process. No matter what your physical experiences are or have been, finding the love within is a personal journey that everyone will take. It can be no other way. Everyone must connect to their fullness. You are more than a brain in a physical body. You are a connection to the whole of all that is. You are connected to forever. The answers to peace are in your connection to self. Learn to love yourself- find the love within. We can tell you that your love within does not come from any relationship that you have had on this physical earth. Whether you have experienced love or disdain in this life time has nothing to do with your love within which is a connection to all that is. It is a connection to infinite love. Learn to spend time with your infinite loving self and watch for changing earth.

YOUR LONGEVITY

We are ready to talk about longevity. We talk about the ability to live a long and joyful life. The idea of course is to live with joy, peace, and love. These over-used terms are really a key to a long and peaceful life. It is no secret that stress takes a toll on the physical body. Stress is the opposite of joy, peace, and love. Perhaps it is time to take those overused terms a bit more seriously. You see, converting the words to action is necessary. You will do this by believing in the outcome and practicing. Let's look a little closer. Peace- the absence of stress. Stress the accumulation of unwanted negative energy. Being off track of your desire. Most of you only know to hold on to the stress and the undesired energy until relief comes along. We say that relief is a choice. Your belief is not a fixed, concrete fact. Your belief is as flexible as your choices. No one is doomed to the unwanted without a choice. That is a fact. Although it may seem like a judgment, you *do* have the power to choose your- overused term- of joy. Your circumstances do not have to predicate your long term emotions. Sure, for awhile you will feel the effect of stressful events. It is your choice, to hold on to the stress or let it go. Your Choice! The overwhelm can feel impossible yet we say that holding on to the feeling of overwhelm- angry, sad, confused, etc. is a choice that creates stress and reduces longevity. Practice releasing, and letting go. Practice knowing that you are connected to a stronger force than anger, sadness, etc. Practice believing in you power to survive a long stress-reduced life.

YOUR BRAIN'S DESIRE AND YOUR HEART'S DESIRE

It is time that you all understand the difference between the desire of your brain and the desire of your heart. All is well when the two are working together. Stress happens when the two are not aligned. Usually the brain wants a specific while the heart is more general. The brain wants a particular person to stay in a particular picture for the purpose of love. The heart accepts all love, starting with self love. The heart- which we mean to be spirit energy, does not set boundaries for whom to love or when. Can you see that the brain is setting limitations which can create stress? Perhaps you might consider adjusting to a larger view of love. Perhaps you can consider allowing different forms of love to pass through your life without limitation. Perhaps you can understand that there will always be love in your life if you are open. You are made of and connected to love. It is your substance. Your brain sets limits on a limitless source. Come to know that truth. Come to accept that you are limitless love and other forms of limitless love will come in and out of your life. There is no need to stress over it.

It is also true that your brain and heart desire abundance. Once again, the brain sets limits while the heart is more general. The brain lives from a belief in limits. The heart- spirit lives in a place of never ending supply. It is time to re-focus your view of prosperity. Instead of living from your brain's experiences and boundaries, live from you spirit's knowledge that there always will be enough for you and everyone else. Adjust your beliefs. Choose to live from your limited brain or from your limitless spirit. Your brain can choose richness, but it may need to align with limitless abundance in spirit energy. Allowing the flow is your choice. Believe in the big picture.

RICH

Now we want to tell you that your purpose is being challenged. For those who live for the purpose of self indulgence, know that there is enough for you and for others. There is no need to hoard. We invite you to have all that you want. We invite you to understand and accept the idea of plentifulness. With this thought, take what is wanted but only what you will use. That is to say, don't kill the forest when you only need a tree. A tree may be useful while the forest may be greed. What is your purpose? Think about it. Ponder your purpose. Is it to create personal wealth at the risk of life on your planet? No one needs to go hungry. No one needs a house which is larger than their need. It is important for you to understand that the feast is for everyone. Come to the table hungry but consume only that which you need. Go with the knowing that the table will always have enough. Live as if you already have it all. You do. *All* is always available for everyone. The idea of possessions and ownership can be challenged. If you see a beautiful painting, do you have to own it, or can you leave it hanging for the enjoyment of all? What we are talking about is the need to possess. What we suggest is take what you need and leave the rest- knowing that there will always be enough.

Further with the talk of wealth, know that there is enough for you and everyone else. We want you to know that no one is singled out to live in poverty or in riches. You may ask how to create richness for all? Richness comes from your connection to all that is. We mean to say that the brain doesn't always have the answer for individual richness but the spirit does. Stop trying to figure it out using negative woe-is-me energy. It won't help. When your brain looks and sees lack, the energy you created is negative- sad, angry etc. Instead look through the eyes of your spirit who has everything. You have everything because you are a part of a rich source. Feel your spiritual richness. That positive energy will then develop into physical richness. First, feel the joy in spiritual richness then see it develop into physical form. While you are tuned in to infinite spiritual richness, take time to also feel infinite love. It's all there- you are infinitely rich and infinitely loved.

BEST TIME, BEST ENERGY

Now is a good time to let you know that the best is coming. We have been telling you how to create the best possible earthly adventures by choosing your energy. Now we will tell you that the best is being created for earth. The messages are growing and the energy is changing. Allow. Allow the growth of positive energy in your life. Not only will you personally benefit but so will all of your planet. Create a habit of tuning into positive energy as often as possible each day. Become aware of the feeling, and then become aware of your changing physical conditions. Become aware of your potential to create a loving, joyful, happy planet for everyone. You have the power, you have the key. We, your guides and teachers, cannot do the physical job of creating the energy of peace. It is our joy and our job to lead you on the path; your job is to create the change. We work together as a team. Our vision is the same as yours. Can you see it? Can you imagine the energy of peace? A good place to start is with imagination. Imagination uses both your brain and your spirit (heart). Hold the vision for days, weeks, and months until it becomes real and believable for you. While doing so, continue to tap into infinite love. FEEL your self love which is coming from an infinite source. You *are* love. You are a part of infinite love which is a part of life. You are alive; therefore you are connected to infinite love. Even the person acting our as 'bad' is connected to infinite love. Now is a good time to sssshs your brain. Notice your breathing- your life. Keep noticing and allow the feeling of love. It will come from your infinite connection. Allow.

Now is the best time to join the best energy. It is beginning to grow around your planet. Join in and contribute to life on your planet. Believe in you power, your purpose, and your contributions.

THE NEW AND THE OLD ENERGIES OF EARTH

It is time to discuss the comings and goings on Earth. We mean the comings and goings of a new world. The comings and goings of change which life has created. Coming is world peace, world happiness. Going is assumed power and control with economic privilege. Coming is a land of freedom for all- without wars, battles, fights or angry words. Coming is a planet of life, love, and peace. You are the life, love, and peace maker. You are valued.

It is clear that power, control, greed, anger, etc., is still around. It is also clear that those negative energies are diminishing. Yes, the negative energy may still be a part of your news programs and personal gossips. One reason negative energy is still talked about is for awareness. People are speaking out and drawing awareness to the separations. Be aware but don't thrive on hearing or speaking negative energy. Be aware that negative energy is coming to light. Don't dwell on it. Don't draw out the process. Instead, notice, express gratitude for the view, then release. Return to your loving self. Hold others in loving light. Everyone is in a role. Everyone is bringing awareness in one way or another. What is your way? Make it personal. Be the energy of change in your own personal way. Your energy is coming, centuries old energy is going. What are you bringing for the next generations?

THE VIEW THROUGH YOUR EXPERIENCES
Let's go ahead with talk of the new Earth. We will describe more of the view.

Imagine streams without pollution. Some of these still exist and some people may remember drinking from them. Imagine a time of food growing in every neighborhood. Imagine a time of sharing because your table is overflowing. Abundance will be normal in every country and every community.

And now imagine peace. Imagine a time of no war and nothing to fight over. Really, there is nothing to fight over because there is plenty for everyone. The idea of power over others will cease to exist. Love for self and others will be the new power. Imagine how much will get done when people work together. Do you see how separation is interrupting progress? Do you see how they-against-them slows advancement? The idea is for Earth to advance into a peaceful thriving planet.

View peace; view a planet whose life forces have joined together in celebration of life. The new leaders will be connected to their truth within. The new followers will be connected to their love-highest energy- within. Everyone will be able to tune in to their infinite connection. The spirit and the brain will work in harmony, each helping the other.

Imagine a world of laughter, joy, and happiness. Oh there will still be times of upset, and times of growth. There will still be times to remember sorrow. Those times will be shorter and less dramatic. Adventures will still happen and still be exciting. But mostly people will want to spend time enjoying life. After all, that is why you are here. It's ok to begin the enjoyment now. Become aware of your good times. Make them last as long as possible, and then create another good time, and another, and another. Begin to view the future- now. View through your experiences.

FEEDING THE ENERGY OF ALL

It is a good time to think about coming together as one. Think of one planet with one energy source. And think of many life forms with the same energy source. It is time to work from your togetherness instead of your separateness. That is to say, work from your infinite connection *and* your separate physical brains. We invite you to become a team with your more knowledgeable self. Then become a team for all of planet Earth. It is a lot easier to join with life then to fight it. Make it easy on yourself. This is an invitation to consciously become aware of and to join with your higher self and the higher self of all. Earth is a part of a magnificent forever. You are a part of the energy of Earth. You create the energy of earth. Can you see how the energies all join together? Can you see your place in the whole of all? Now can you understand that your job is to create the best energy for you, Earth, and forever? All is one and you are an energy source. Your positive energy is feed for all. We ask that you create with consciousness the positive energy that will flow through all that is. Continue with bringing life to all that is. Life is created with positive energy; the best, strongest, and most powerful is the energy of love.

THE PROCESS OF CREATING YOUR DESIRE

We will tell you about the creation process. Whatever you choose to create is within your power. Creation is channeling your energy. We strongly suggest that you begin by letting go. If you are surrounding yourself and holding on to worry, sadness, or any negative energy, we suggest that you release it. Simply drop your shoulders, release the tightness in your neck, let go. Those energies were reinforcing that which you did not want. While you are letting go, also silence your brain of negative thoughts. Ssshs. Just stop the self-talk. Take a breath. Allow a positive energy to enter the recently vacuumed space. The more positive you allow to enter, the more positive your life will become. Begin to believe in the scene you are creating. Believe it before you can see it. Believe in the plan while the seed is in the soil. As you look around, begin to give thanks for the vision of your new creation. Begin to know that you have the power to create by channeling your energy. That is the process. Practice. Over time, the process will be without effort. Practice regularly.

NOW IS THE TIME OF CHANGE

We really want you to know- it is important to know- that now is the time of change. Now is the time to see a beautiful picture.

Now is the time to see the picture of peace. It is your time on Earth. Those of you who are alive in physical form are here to begin the revolution into peace. You may notice the ruckus, the discord, the unsettlement. Be assured that the negative energy is coming into light. Once in light, in conscious awareness, issues can be dealt with. Negative energy can be turned into positive energy much quicker with awareness.

The brunt of the burden of change is with the Now generation. It is now that the energy of change is with earth. Oh Earth has always been changing, yet now Earth is going into its transition of peace. If you look for it, you will see it. Look past the norm. Look into areas you haven't seen before. Look for new understandings. Look for a change in religions. Look for acceptance of all ideas, and not coveted, limited or secular ideas and beliefs.

Now is the time of change and progress into a peaceful Earth. Come together to recognize the strongest energy source of love. All you have to do is live in love, joy, happiness, and all the other positive energies. Live in the awareness of infinite truth. Each of you will awaken in your own time. Practice now to question, to explore in your mind. Simply look around and see beyond your limited brain thinking. Now is the time to see a beautiful picture. Imagine, create, and see the peace. Now.

WHAT TO DO WHILE THE SEED SPROUTS

We recognize that anxiety may build while waiting for a specific outcome. We know that you ask and expect, almost in the same breath. A miracle? When all the energies are in alignment the miracle will happen. Until then, there is a movement of energy which can be a movement of beliefs, awareness, knowing, etc.... Planting the seed means developing the thought, the idea, the belief, the truth, the knowing.... Sprouting happens as your energy aligns with the seed of thought. How long will it take you to disconnect from old beliefs? How much time do you need to connect with your infinite knowledge? That is how long it will take for the seed to sprout, become visible, and bear flowers of fruit. An instant, a day, a year, a life time? It's up to you.

What to do while you wait? Create the environment of knowing. Live as if. Know- that which you seek is here. Always was, always will be. Are you ready? Understand that you are of purpose and your purpose is not to suffer. Your purpose is to expand love, joy, happiness, etc.

While the seed sprouts, be that which you wish to develop. Be peace. Be the outcome of your desire. Be joy.

BE AWARE OF YOUR IMPORTANCE

Now we will talk about forever more. For you, your children, and their children. You are here creating your future. Each generation is creating the future of the next generations. Your energy will live on- forever. Even if you don't have children, your energy lives on just as your parents energy does. For your energy to live on through time, you won't need to stay in a body. Your energy, outside of the body, is creating waves of future energy. Both waves of growth and waves of devastation are being channeled through you. Either way, your energy is flowing from you in to waves of forever. Because you are in physical form, you have the mass to alter waves of energy. Take this as an important mission. *You* are important to the future of earth. We can imagine that most of you don't realize your importance. We see you unconsciously creating without awareness. We would like to enlighten you. Always, you are a wave of either positive or negative energy- depending on your thoughts, beliefs, and behaviors.

And now, we invite you to become aware of the energy you emit. More often than not, become aware of emitting positive energy. Of course low frequency energy will still be a part of you, but choose to dominate with high energy frequency HEF. Bring awareness, become conscious of the number of times during a day that you are in LEF (low energy frequency) and the number of times you are in HEF. Work with it, play with it, direct your energy frequencies. Yes, you can. You are important.

The energy of millions of years is being channeled through you. Direct it in favor of future earth. You can do this. It is an important job and you are here on Earth Now, to handle this mission. We believe in you and we are always here to help. Just in case you're doubting your importance, be reminded that all you need is a physical body, your connection to all that is, and your thoughts, beliefs, and actions. Now, live joyfully, from your loving self.

YOUR PURPOSE IS TO CELEBRATE
Now is the time to start the celebration. You have the knowledge and you have our words. It is your turn to begin living in joy, love, peace, happiness, with smiles, hugs, sharing, generosity... you get the idea. Now is a good time to start. For no particular reason, begin the celebration of sending waves of HEF into the world and into forever. You don't need to direct the energy towards another physical person. You are the creator, now create and send into forever. Channel the river of energy; choose the path of a continuing Earth. Begin now to create a peaceful earth. Begin by being. It is alright to be the odd person with the big smile. It is alright to be the nice person in a group of gloom. Change the river. Be the change that others look for. Be the direction of peace. And have fun with it. Play around, laugh, skip and dance. Break the rules of gloom. Grin at yourself while you are being joyful, silly, and happy. Grin because of awareness that

you are changing the course of future earth and future forever. Grin at your happy importance.

Now you are on board. Now you are with the plan. Keep the party in your heart as long as you have a body. When life gets down for you, ride it out quickly then get back to the celebration of joy. Soon you will find out that the down time gets less and less. Bad stuff just won't shake your world like it once did. Smile and give thanks for all the good stuff you will be experiencing. Now is the time to celebrate. If not now, then when? You are in body. Act as if you have an important purpose. Celebrate.

YOUR TIME FOR THE LIFE TIME

We'll talk about the timing of life and the timing of the end of physical life. In other words, let's talk about physical change. In this ever swirling, ever moving space, there is a time to enter a physical realm and a time to leave the physical realm. Every swirl is taking and leaving physical particles. This is true for the plant, the person, the rock, and the planet. Now is the time for planet Earth to blossom in life. To do so, your energy is necessary. Are you understanding that your positive energy is the creator of life?

We want you to know that having a live prosperous abundant planet is not a guarantee. Instead, it comes from intent. Somewhere, someone, something creates positive energy of life. The grasses, the flowers, the trees... the plants contribute to positive energy. So do the animals that kill for survival. Taking and consuming only what is necessary. The time is coming for awareness of life and death on Earth; positive and negative energy on Earth. Instincts of the past millions of years are changing and developing towards an abundant planet. It is time for humans to do their part. In the tide and flow of physical existence, Earth can have billions of more years. Or humans can devastate and kill off life within your life time.

We are just letting you know that there is a fork in the road. You- humans- are at the fork. It is decision time. What is your view? Your thoughts, your beliefs, and your actions will present the outcome of Earth. Your energy will match with other energies both on planet Earth and in space. On Earth and in space, there is plenty of the energy of life, the energy of love Now is a good time to feed into the swirls of loving positive energy. Your time is now. Be aware.

THE DESIGN OF MATURATION
It is time for maturation of the planet, the people, and all life on Earth. It is time for Earth to mature and move into the next phase. I think many people on earth are getting tired of and bored with the negative energy behaviors. We see signs and bubbles of desire for peace, joy, happiness and love towards one another. What a pleasant sight it is. So refreshing and joyful. To be sure, shall we say... these joy bubbles... are displaced randomly across the world, with their lights coming on, then going off. We look forward to seeing many more signs, and lights of love. Actually, we hope to see the infiltration of Earth with loving joy bubble light energy. What a spectacular sight that will be. Can you imagine it? Billions of love and joy energies shooting across the country at once. Oh we see it. We see the energy of earth. We see the difference each and every individual creates. It isn't difficult for us to imagine because we know the power of every person. We know that everyone is connected to infinite love. We know also, that as each person consciously tunes in and consciously creates joy, laughter, love and happiness, the lights around earth will grow in magnitude. As this happens, earth enters further into the maturation process.

As a mature planet, disease will become remote- so will poverty, murders, judgments, etc. A mature planet is something to look forward to. Helping the planet may be your legacy. But if it isn't, still create all the grins, smiles, loves, and songs that you can. Become a part or the process. Age with design.

A REBELLION

Let's plan a rebellion. That sounds like fun. Let's plan a fun rebellion of joy. The purpose would be to break away from doubt, suspicion, judgments, blame, anger... you get the picture. While in a joyful rebellious way, celebrate the freedom of abundance. We think that is a good idea. For no particular reason, gather with others to hoot and holler about joyfulness, and playfulness. Rebel against the control of fearful ways —all of them. Now is a good time to let it be known that freedom, love, joy, happiness is in everyone's best interest. Let it be known that now is a perfect time to sound the trumpet for world peace and love.

With your time and talent, how can you see your rebellion? Can you see yourself acting alone by expressing kindness? Can you see yourself joining with others to help others? Can you see yourself organizing a community to make changes for the sake of all? How about, if you are a leader, can you see yourself organizing major changes in your state, or country?

Let me help with the vision- Can you see the end of prisons? Can you see the end of homelessness? Can you see the end of war? How are those visions working for you? Can you help feed even one person or carry a load for just one person?

Now is a good time to begin your rebellion. Start with feeling good, feeling, joyful, feeling your connection to endless love. Now share the feeling. There, you did it. You visualized your rebellion. We are with you moving into action.

74

MORE REBELLING

While we are out stirring energy of change, let's also change the news; those programming messages that tear us apart with bitterness, hate, sadness, or distain. It is time to listen to broadcasts of joining. Who is your announcer or what is your source of written news? We aren't saying that all the news needs to be replaced; we are saying that it certainly needs to be tweaked. How many ways can one subject be discussed? (Hint- these books of Now are all talking about the same thing- peace and love.) If the "subject" is your leader, how many ways can you mention his/her faults, weaknesses, style, and so forth? Can you imagine talking about that person's strength instead of weaknesses. Can you imagine making it news worthy? Try. Try going into your place of infinite love, take this leader with you, now connect. It can be done. See that on a deeper spiritual level, you are both made from love.

Now rebel against the negative news sources. Don't listen, don't watch, don't read. Choose your entertainment. Find a news that will create a smile. How is that for rebelling! Work at it. Work at finding or creating a news source that is centered around positive contributions. Do yourself a favor, rebel against that which isn't bringing you joy.

We invite you to be a rebel of good news. Practice.

YOU ARE A BROADCASTER OF NEWS

The good news is that you are here on earth to create goodness. Now that is good news. We encourage you to share the news of your purpose. You can share the good news in many ways. Share through writing about good stuff. Share through reading good stuff. Share through the performing arts of good entertainment.

Of course a wonderful way of sharing your good news is to be. Be joyful, funny, happy, loving. Be playful, and laugh a lot. Be the good news for others to see. By doing so, your personal news program will be shared through all of time and throughout the entire universe. Your news program will be shared through the positive energy that you send out, and that others send out because they tuned in to your broadcast.

Are you aware of your constant broadcasting? Tune in to what you are saying, doing, and absorbing. Now is a good time to view yourself as the broadcaster of news. You are. You are always broadcasting on frequencies that travel into forever. Is it time to analyze your script? We think so. Take a good look at your broadcasts. If you like what you see, then give thanks to yourself for a job well done. Congratulate yourself to encourage more of the same. If you don't like what you see, then make a few tweaks and resend. It is never too late to send powerful messages of goodness. We think this is good news worth writing about.

EARTH'S TRANSITION TO PEACE

The topic now is transitioning to peace. Transitioning to peace is an unfolding of new ways of being. Being- is a way of thinking, believing, and acting. It seems as though there is a lot of pre-programmed ways of being and most of the time, people don't challenge the programming. So let me shake it up a bit. I'll be the one to challenge the program. Now is a good time to take a closer look at why you think, believe, and act the way you do. We aren't saying its right or wrong, we are asking you to take a look.

In your way of being, do you exclude or include other individuals, groups, countries...? Somewhere in your past, maybe now unconscious, did you learn to judge others as good or bad, acceptable or unacceptable, worthy or unworthy? The answer is, of course you did. Others have different beliefs and they share those beliefs. Then if you believe what the other said, then you are picking up on a judgment.

Right or wrong, good or bad, everyone picks up on what others say-think-act.

My question is, are those ways of being, in line with the joy, love, happiness of all? It is now time to look deeper inside yourself. Tune in to your truth within. The deeper part of you which is connected to all that is. We say deeper, because tuning in to all that is- your inner truth, is less shallow more knowing than your limited brain. This isn't a judgment, it is a truth that your brain knows a lot of its physical existence and your spirit knows a lot of its forever existence.

It is time to challenge your source of information because it is time to transition into a peaceful, loving, earth. If your information is not for the betterment of all, then you are receiving non-peaceful information for all. The entire planet can transition into peace when everyone is included. Everyone-includes a transition for the good guy and the bad guy, the wanted and the not wanted. The transition is for everyone on Earth.

LOOK DEEPER INTO THE IDEA OF JUSTICE

Reasonable Justice. Most people want "justice" after an assumed wrong has been done. I say "assumed wrong" because there are probably different opinions as to the right or wrong of a situation. Also there is probably different information leading up to the cause. Therefore it is suggested that you look a little deeper into the justice. We suggest that you look further than you-killed-so-you-get-killed-in-return. In other words, look further into the idea of an-eye-for-an-eye. Having more dead people or more blind people may not be justice. Instead of *more* consider the idea of *less*. Less revenge-justice, and more compassion. You see, revenge-justice will prolong a society of *injustices*. Once again we are going with the idea that you are all one. Everyone comes from the same source, and everyone is connected to the highest energy frequency of life/love. Therefore, everyone can be a positive contributor in your society- unless your justice system prolongs an assumed injustice. Am I making sense? Are you beginning to understand how people are contributing to negative energy by your society's reaction to an assumed injustice? If you want the pot of water to be less salty, you don't add more salt. Instead you would dilute by adding more water.

Dilute the negative behavior. Keep adding more positive energy and less negative energy to the unjust situation. Create a justice for all. We understand that you want to be angry with the person who committed the crime. When you come to understand *your* emotion, realize that going forth with more anger, fear, sadness, or revenge will not create a positive society. Putting out the match won't put out all the fires. Re-align with your truth within, then see that the "wrong doer" also realigns with the truth within. Only by realigning with inner peace, inner love, inner truth will justice be served. It can be no other way.

NOW IS YOUR TIME TO CREATE PEACE

It has come to our attention that timing is necessary. In order to create change in your world, begin an action. Create a thought or vision of peace, create a belief that peace can and *will* happen. If you need inspiration, look at the peace around you. It is there, mixed in with the non-peace. Where is your focus? Focus on what you want to see and create. Focus on the good stuff. Now, create more of that good stuff. Plant more flowers, walk more dogs, smile with more children. Well, you get the idea. As often as possible, act with positive energy. There, is that simple enough?

We think so. Bring conscious awareness to your actions. We are asking you to know about the energy you emit.

While you are changing to conscious awareness, you are also changing the energy surrounding your planet. Now is the time for this job. You are here. Your turn is now. Make the very best of your time in physical form. The very best is peace, love, joy, happiness. That means, laugh a lot, and take a break from the mundane. Kick your life up a notch by bringing awareness to you smiles and laughter. Live with purpose, and the purpose is peace. Now is your time. We know you can do it.

THE CHANGING TIMES ARE LEADING BACK TO PEACE

There was a time on Earth when peace was dominant. That was long ago before life as you know it. Then came the age of competition to survive. This is the age that your current historians or archeologist now study. However, way back, long ago, there was peace. Earth has always been able to maintain life. There has always been enough. Still competition grew. As it grew, so did greed and destruction, along with slavery. This also brought on the time of empires and fights over land rights. Now we have the present; a time where the idea of peace is once again beginning to develop. Of course there will be struggle during this developing peace. The struggles will mostly begin in the brains of those who don't know any other way except competition. Some people are good competitors, others are not. Some are good peacemakers, others are not. This will be a time to look deeper within for the answers. Those who have and those who have not will begin to look within- mostly by necessity. The time will come when one group will not support the other group. Everyone will learn of their own value and inner strength on a planet of plenty.

The good news is that more sharing will happen. It will be perfectly normal to help each other and be helped in return. Can you imagine the end of homelessness, the end of starvation, and the end of brutality? Try. Just for a few moments try to visualize. In those few moments of visualization, you produced world changing energy. Keep visualizing regularly. Talk about it. Visualize with others. Now, a lot of world energy is changing. It has to start somewhere. Let be with you.

NOW IS THE TIME TO TAKE ACTIONS OF PEACE

There is a bit of urgency. We want to express a concern to begin with peace NOW. Now is your time of action. Now is when Earth is most ready for your action of peace. Creativity? Do you need to be more creative in finding peaceful ways of being with each other? Maybe so. Maybe start with identifying something you would like to change, excessive murders, depression, homelessness... the list goes on. Choose one, focus and visualize an outcome. Become one with the vision. Begin to see change. You don't have to make this difficult. Just follow your vision. No matter how large or small, begin to move the mountain of negative energy. The way to do this is with loving, caring, joyful energy.

I can see the change that is coming. I see the changing energy. If you planted the seed, keep feeding it with your positive energy. Believe in your ability to create change. If not you, then who? The movement has started, the path is prepared. Now it is your turn. We will be with you... always. Lovingly, caring, joyfully believing in you.

YOUR TIME YOUR TURN

This is your turn. Now is your time because you are here in physical body and you are moving energy. Your conscious awareness and deliberate action is what we are asking for. We, The Teaches of Life and Love are here to help you so that you can help Earth transition to a planet of positive loving, caring, joyful, energy; the energy of survival. The messages from all of us Teachers throughout time have always been the same. LOVE. We bring forth the message of love which is the message of life. Now is the time for your planet to thrive. You the inhabitants have the job of keeping Earth alive. You do this through your actions, which come from your thoughts and beliefs, both conscious and unconscious. There is no escaping this truth. You may want to hide from the truth or blame others for your actions, yet *you* are the responsible person for the energy that you send and receive from infinite space. Because you are the one who is responsible, we ask that you use your responsibility wisely, and knowingly. Become aware of your thoughts, beliefs, and actions. Become aware of your intent and your purpose. Know that you are the creator of the energy that comes and goes through you.

Become aware of your use of love and fear, which also means kindness, joy, happiness or hate, anger, depression. You all are the leaders of Earth's future. Don't lead blindly. Lead in the light of awareness. Be aware of when you smile and when you frown. Mostly, be aware of love from within. Your loving connection to infinite self- god, source, the whole of all, will always be a part of you. Make it your friend. Learn to find and tune into that part of you. Your self-love may be buried under layers of abuse. Dig it out. Unbury the light of love inside of you. Once you do, the miracles of joy, physical love, and abundance will be with you. Allow. Heal. Find your loving inner self. This is your time, your turn.

NOW IS YOUR TIME TO CREATE THE CHANGE
Are you getting it? Are you understanding the messages and your reason for being on Earth in a physical body? We will tell you that the only time you have, is now while you are in body. Once you release your body, your mass will not be dense enough

to create the energy changes that are needed to sustain the movement. Therefore, use your time in body for the greatest cause. Use your time in body to create a loving world. Make a point of smiling more, and enjoying more. Sing and dance. Feel the joy. More. Turn in up a notch. We know you won't be in HEF all the time. We know that you will cycle in and out. Conscious awareness will help. Find a way to stir your memory and remind yourself regularly of your purpose. Practice. Eventually the practice will become a habit.

While you are at it, practice finding and tuning into the love within. The love from infinite source is your survival- your life line. Forever. Get peaceful, breathe in to your heart area. Imagine your infinite love. You *are* love. Give thanks. Are you getting it?

NOW IS YOUR TURN

We are pleased with the progress being made. We see the wheels turning and we see the change happening. Even though it may not look like progress, some of the events are necessary to bring the awareness that will create the change. Believe. Know that the unwanted will be brought to light. Know that peace will come from the chaos. Know too that new pockets of peace have already formed. Know this because some people had the belief which created the change. Now it is your turn. Join with others in creating peace. The joining will intensify your progress. Now is your turn to implement your plan of peace. Listen inside until you hear the plan. However large or small your part will be, now is the time to implement. You will know the plan is right because it will feel good. When you feel good, happy, loving joyful, you are on the right path to peace. In your home, your relationships, your job, your world, be there with joy. If not joy, then you might be in the wrong place. If you are in a good place, but can't feel the joy, you may not be in a good place with yourself. You probably need to find the loving connection to infinite self. Once you do, it will take you to all the right places- of joy, happiness, love. Now is your turn for your hearts connection to its infinite loving source. That is the right place, now is the right time.

BELIEFS 1

We would like to introduce you to a new or different perspective. Being introduced to different ideas helps with developing beliefs. Quite often, once someone develops a belief, it can be difficult to change. The difficulty is in the attachment to the belief. Try for a moment to un-attach to something you belief. Notice the bantering in your head. Notice the separation fear? This little exercise is to help with awareness. Are you willing to deepen your awareness of your beliefs? Let's just say, are you willing to reassess your beliefs; look closer in to how they came to be? Are your beliefs for the benefit of one or everyone?

As we said before, beliefs are changeable. They are not meant to be permanent. Now may be a good time to view a change? Our suggestion is to be flexible with your beliefs. Whatever your subject or belief, is it negotiable? If you want to stick solidly to something, stick solidly to a kindness, a goodness, a joyfulness, a funfulness. Let all other arguments go. Be prepared to release what you don't need.

BELIEFS 2

Let us continue with letting go of beliefs. What we are asking is that you take a deeper look at why you believe the way you do. How is it helping you or others? Do you believe in violent acts? Can you justify your beliefs? Look deeper, a violent act is war. Do you believe in war- in a home, a neighborhood, a country or- war within yourself? Be the spokesperson for your belief. Look deeper into why you believe a particular way before joining an argument about it. Take the time to examine. Take the time to look for a peaceful resolution. If there is a belief which others may argue, then take the time to humbly challenge your position. What we are saying is, accept that your beliefs may be different from the beliefs of other persons. Accept that wars can be fought over differences in beliefs. Is it worth the battle- verbal or physical? Look deeper. What can you let go of once you find its origin? What do you want to hold most sacred above all else? Take some time. Look for the value in your belief.

BELIEFS 3

It is important to know that your beliefs are an energy that you emit. Your beliefs work on energy frequencies. That shouldn't be difficult to understand. Your beliefs- your energy- create. That is why we ask you to become aware of your beliefs. YOU have the power through thought, belief, and action to create a situation. The creation may not be just as you imagined it, because you probably didn't knowingly create as an energy wave. What we want you to know is that you are always creating, become aware. Guide your creations. If you are wanting sunshine but mostly think of the dreary cloudy days, you will probably get more dreary cloudy. If you are wanting less mass murders but are thinking of guns, and shootings, you will probably witness or hear about more shootings.

Imagine what you want to be created. There is no one else to blame for your creation. Pay attention. Imagine, think, believe, and act purposely. Know that you are a creator, the contributor to your planet by the energy you emit. Think about it before emitting. That is what we want you to know.

KEEP YOUR FOCUS ON PEACE

Next we will discuss the abilities to alter creations. You might want to know how to go about altering the negative energy on Earth. That is to say that you may want to decrease illness, poverty, loneliness, and all other negative energies. Let me tell you that beyond a doubt this is possible. It seems clear to us that it is possible. If you look around, can you also see the possibilities. Try. Imagine positive energy being emitted all across Earth. Imagine that the abundance of positive energy is creating more health, abundance, and love. It really isn't that difficult to understand. Imagine that negative energy is creating negative circumstances. Try to think of it in terms of you being the driver in the bus. You are in control. No matter how much noise is going on in the seats behind you, keep your focus on the path- the road to where the spirit of all wants to be. The spirit of all is connected to all, therefore the spirit of all will be travelling to peace. Keep your focus on peace. Whatever your endeavors and whatever is going on in the news or in the world, keep your focus on peace. We are suggesting that you don't draw lines of rejection or acceptance. We are suggesting that your team and their team probably want to win world peace. It is all a matter of planning the game. The game is Peace on Earth. It can't be won without one unity, without one agreement, and without one love. Peace doesn't come with divided interest. Peace comes from an interest in everyone being a winner. All of earth wins when everyone believes that it can be. This will take time. It starts with one belief. Let it start with you.

HEALING STARTS WITH DESIRE

Now it is time we share words of joy, words of hope, and words of wisdom. It is our great pleasure to present an accumulation of thoughts. These thoughts are on helpful words in times of troubled heart. Our thoughts on troubled hearts, or troubled emotions begin with saying that your spirit is on a journey. All journeys are in motion, therefore you will be moving through troubled times, not staying there. Visualize a path. A walk on the path, a stumble and fall on the path. We suspect that you won't stay on the fall. We suspect that when you are ready, you will get up and continue. View this as guide for the discomforts in your life. The path goes on and so will you. Your spiritual path will last many life times. There will be many stumbles as you venture on to ultimate peace and love. The speed is up to you; always has been and always will be. You can sit in your stumble for minutes or for centuries. Eventually, you will move on- when you are willing. We aren't discounting the severity of the stumble or the degree of pain it may cause. We know of the pain and suffering. Keep in mind that you are never alone during these times. Always, always, there are spirits with you who love you deeply. Always these spirits feel your suffering. And always these spirits wait for you to be on your path again. On your path and walking with loving peace. Always.

Sometimes we hear that you don't know the path or you can't find the path. Let us say that you are *always* on the path. You may *think* that you are lost. That is an illusion. You are on the path and your loving spirit guides are always with you. If your life feels like hell, move on. You can do this by acknowledging your wounds. Acknowledge that things happened. For each 'happening' allow the tears, that clean your wounds. Allow the letting go. Know that you don't have to stay stuck in your hell. Know that peace and love are a part of you. Know that you can let go and move past the hell. Stay in your stumble or move out of it. Your choice. Even if you don't know what love and peace feel like, you can still move out of your hell. Argue with me or accept our words. Your choice. We know that when you are ready, you will move on to the peace and love which your heart desires. It is peace, love, and joy that you wish for- even if you don't understand. The journey begins with a change of desire, a change in consciousness. Practice desiring peace, love, and joy. Desire is a good place to start.

YOU ARE LOVE

Let's start by saying that whoever and wherever you are on the planet, you are love. Whether you feel like love or hate, you are love. That is because you have the highest energy frequency within you. HEF, known to people on earth as love, god, source, etc, is a part of your make-up. It is the make-up of your spirit and your spirit is infinite, therefore you are made of infinite love. Just thought you might want to know this. There will be times when you don't feel the love within yet it is still there. The love within is still available for everyone, at all times- anytime you choose to tune in and connect with it. The love, the high energy frequency is life. You are a part of life. You can't be good enough or bad enough to have or have not the love within. What you might want to do is practice tuning in- looking for it, feeling it, living from that place.

And now, practice surrendering all that is not love. For a moment or as long as you can, surrender your negative energy. Let it go. Feel the void, the empty space. We think it is a peaceful restful place. When you are ready, allow love to enter that space. Allow. Give permission. For a moment or as long as you can hold it, allow love to fill the space. Practice regularly.

When the tears flow, healing is happening.

IN LOVING HEALTH

Now, we will talk about Health. If you have healed, you have prepared for health. Good health comes from healed wounds. They affect each other. Now, know that your physical health is dependent on your spiritual health. There is much to be said about physical health. Be ready to adjust your thoughts and beliefs.

Be ready to accept a new or different way of thinking. Accept that you have more control over your physical health then might have been imagined. Accept that you have more control than does the food you eat or the exercise you get. Accept that your connection to loving self has the most control over your health. That is probably not too surprising because your loving self is the highest energy frequency available. Your love within and your connection to infinite love is the most powerful force available. Use it to heal.

Your loving self, loving connection, is meant to be used. It is present to serve the spiritual and the physical body. Would you like the miracle pill? It is called love. Take a dose regularly.

We hear the doubt. We understand you can't believe that self love, feeling the love within, infinite love... will cure terminal illness. If your spirit is ready to be free of the body, then no, there will be no cure. If your body is sick because of negative energy, then yes, love will heal. Love will guide you towards healing. How would you know the difference? Either way, die with love, and live with love. Love is the answer to illness. Let it be.

NOW IS YOUR DAY

Now we will write about the comings and goings of your world, and your thoughts. One affects the other. It is time to hear about the differences that you make. The differences are because of you, and the energy that you put out. Listen. Plan. Think about your capabilities. All of you, everyone is a valued part of the energy of earth. Become aware of what *you* are creating. YOU, not them.

Now is the time to see your creation. Look around. What is your view? What do you want to keep and what do you want to let go of? Now is your time- while you are in body. We have a suggestion. View goodness. Look for the goodness in yourself. Magnify it. Make it glow. It is your turn. Now is your day. What's your plan? -Just a reminder of your greatness.

MAKE LIFE EASIER ON YOURSELF

We are here to announce the coming of greatness. We are here with words for the people. Our messages are about the greatest potential you have. Your greatest potential is your energy of love. Use it. Take advantage of the best resource available to you. What we are saying is to make life easier. Let go of the drama. Now is the time to recognize the energy of love. Again, we don't mean a loving relationship with another person. We are talking about your connection to infinite love which is your source of life both physical and spiritual. We want you to make it easy on yourself. To make life easier, live from you greatest power, not from your weakest. Be assured that both positive and negative frequencies exist. You get to choose the amount of time to stay in both.

Now let's make sense of this. We are saying that you have a choice of how difficult or easy life can be. We are saying that living from positive energy is the most efficient and easiest way to live in physical body. Living in negative energy is more difficult with more obstacles, and more suffering. Both energies will be available to you. It will be your choice as to how much time your will spend either in positive or negative energy. With this in mind, choose your path. Even when 'bad' things happen, how deep do you want to be in the badness? How quickly will you want to be out of badness? All you have to do is become aware, and create a change. Let go of the pain, sorrow, anger, etc, and tune in to goodness. Know that the negative energy is temporary and you can pass through as quickly or as slowly as you chose. Life in greatness comes from living in positive energy.

WHO YOU ARE IS THE SAME AS THEM

It is time for a further discovery. This time we will be talking about the discovery of self. Who are you? What makes you the same and different from another. Why did you choose, before birth, to look the way you do. Does it help with your purpose?

We will answer some questions about the wonderfulness of *you*. Everyone in physical form has dressed for the occasion. That is to say that your physical appearance is suited for your position in life. Your position is to achieve towards the love which you came from; spiritual growth to the electro energy life then the energy of the whole. We will be talking more of this energy in the next book. For now, know that your appearance in this bodily time is giving you the opportunity to grow in spirit. Whatever your spiritual path is about, you are dressed in the most suited body for your journey. Instead of pointing out the beauties or the ugliness in each other, you would be better off to know that each body is designed for the purpose of the spirit within. Over many life times, everyone will have the opportunity to wear different bodies, and be in different roles. It is all a part of the journey. You all are a loving part of the whole. Everyone is the same... in different bodies.

REAL VERSES NON-REAL OF HEALING

Now let's talk about the real verses the non-real of the physical condition. By real, we mean a real physical body which is made up of energy. Little particles of energy, all squeezed together to form one mass of ever changing form. The non-real of the physical body is about its short journey through time. Imagine, if you can, a physical form with the ability to reconstruct and alter itself. Such is the human body. You see, the body is designed for changeability to accommodate growth. To be clearer, the body is capable of self healing and self repair. In the future, there will be more practice of healing the body through a spiritual place of love. Mostly, people aren't ready right now. As humans begin relying more on their spiritual inner truth, connection to the whole... to infinite love, then the ability to self heal through these channels will happen. For now, know this as a truth. Talk about self healing as a truth and as a possibility. We would like for you all to begin getting used to the idea.

Self healing is possible because everyone is connected to the truths of forever. To start, practice, listening within, ask within, surrender within, and allow from within. Better yet, become one with within. In time, this will start making sense. For now, hear the words and know that real healing comes from inside. Non-real healing is covering the wound; sometimes know as the bandage effect. Cover the wound, try not notice, medicate with your choice of what keeps you from noticing the pain within. The pain is separation from the whole. The real fix is with the reconnect.

DIRECTING YOUR FOREVER ENERGY

Now is a day for new words of growth and discovery. We will share more truths for you to discover. Now, the truth of forever. The reason that you will participate in forever is because you have energy. All energy participates in forever. Endless time. Your separate particles of energy, when combined, produce the whole of all that is. Confusing? In simple terms, you are a particle of forever. Your body will transform, recycle, and forever be a part of endless time. So will your spirit- the lighter, less dense part of you. Your body and spirit can and will change, but you- your energy will not poof into nothing.

Since your energy will be here for always, we suggest you direct it for the greater good. How about directing your energy towards peace? It is possible, and peace will come only when people like you believe it can happen. We aren't asking you to change the world. Just yourself. If everyone begins to change themselves, planet Earth will become peaceful. One person, one snowflake, one grain of sand. Be the person who brightens the planet and paves a path to peace. Use your endless energy and your recycled forever body, for the greater good of peace. Now is your time to make this happen.

THE NECESSITY OF CHANGE

Now we are ready to talk about the necessities. It is very clear that you will be engaged in change. Remember that change always happens. All energy is in constant motion. Our suggestion is that you don't try forcing a standstill. It won't happen. Your best plan would be to join the flow of positive energy. What we are saying is that it will be necessary for everyone to open their minds to new ways of thinking, and being. Be open. Allow differences.

Now is a good time to challenge beliefs, and question assertions. Don't get to comfortable in a know-it-all way of being. Your brain can never know it all, therefore don't get stuck with an assumption of being right. We are saying this because it will be necessary for people to change. It will be necessary for people to let go of negative energy so that the positive energy of peace can come through. Try it. Practice daily. Pay attention to your thoughts, words, and behaviors. Let go of the negative, insert a positive. These words are written to help you with awareness. Challenging the messenger or the message will not bring peace. Peace will come from within. These words are meant for direction and guidance. Peace is a necessity.

A MESSAGE FOR BEGINNERS

This message is for beginners. If you are a beginner to spiritual thinking, then you might need a bit more guidance. Let me say that probably- quite likely, your resistance will be about believing. We understand. It is difficult to believe what you can't understand through five senses. What we suggest is that you begin with looking for other "things" that you can't experience with five senses. A few examples are bacteria, distant planets, and neurons. Mostly, these things weren't believed before microscopes were invented. Microscopes are to aid the limited vision of physical eyes. We are suggesting that you open your thoughts and imagination to unlimited visions. Imagine that the source of your liveliness is an energy of love. So far- so good. That shouldn't be too difficult, even if you don't experience love- infinite love, it is still present. As you progress in your spiritual thinking, the idea of infinite love will seem more plausible. As you progress, you will begin to believe and understand that love=life. For now, know that more exists past your five senses. You may need, a microphone, a microscope, or a messenger with words to enhance your reality- your beliefs. We all had to begin somewhere. We welcome you to further exploration in the unseen.

SEEING THE BEAUTY

Let's see more beauty. Now, is a good time to talk about beauty. It is in your scope, your vision, your ability to see beauty. You won't be needing a magnifier except through your desire. We encourage you to magnify the beauty in your world. Of course everyone stares at sunsets and flowers. Now is a good time to stare through the beauty of love- high frequency, infinite love. You see, it is through love, joy, and happiness... that you witness the physical beauty in your world. Beauty may become invisible during times of anger, sadness, and low frequency. We invite you to take time while in low frequency to search for beauty. Raise your frequencies by looking at beauty. Take a few moments, to create beauty in your world.

Seeing the beauty is a choice. Beauty is available to everyone at all times. See without eyes, see through the inner eyes of love. We want you to know that beauty comes from within. The rose, and the sunset is beautiful only if your heart- your love chooses to see it as such.

UNDERSTANDING YOUR CONTRIBUTIONS

We are ready to talk more about the view of a peaceful world. Can you imagine? Try. Imagine a world where everyone gets along through understanding. Imagine the view of everyone understanding the source of poverty, violence, hatred, fear, etc. Imagine that, because everyone can understand, everyone is willing to act through a peaceful understanding. We see it. We can imagine it and so can you. In time, it will be. For now, we are asking that you start in that direction.

More often than not look for understanding. With those whom you dislike, look for a different view. Look to understand what causes the person you dislike to act the way they do. Underneath all the looking will be the view of love. The bad, unlikeable person has love at the core. That person is acting in a way that training, has led towards. The person who murders has been trained by a society. The person who steals has been trained by a society; so has the person who hoards, hates, and harms.

It is time to look at a peaceful society. It is time to understand how a fear-based society cannot create a love-based society. Go inside, to your love within. Breathe into an understanding of your contributions. How often do live with loving understanding?

How often do live in judgment? This is a reminder of your contribution to the bad person *and* the good person. Every person on Earth contributes to the energy of Earth and beyond. Begin to understand your part of all this. Begin to make adjustments.

LIKELINESS OF ONE PEACEFUL PLANET

It is time to consider the likeliness of coming together as one peaceful planet. For everyone, there is opportunity to contribute. You are here on earth with the ability to move mountains of peace, love, hatred, and fear. It is while you are here that change is happening. We are pleased to say that many people are waking up to the idea of peace. Many people are raising high energy frequencies. What about you? More often than not, what is your energy frequency? More often than not, do you see the beauty or the ugly? Do you often experience the self love or the self hate?

We encourage you to look for the beauty, the joy, and the self love. We encourage you to move the mountain into high energy frequencies of sustainable life. Of course, it is always your choice. Become aware of your choices and the direction your energy is moving. The more awareness you have, the more choices you will have. Your time on Earth is now. What is the likeliness of you contributing to peace?

GETTING TO THE ANSWERS WITHIN

Now is a good time to discover the truths of you. We will talk about the deeper levels of truth that you have. Because everyone is connected to all that is, everyone has access to all that is. Of course you in your physical, time restricted brain can't access, but just imagine your connection to all that is. In your imagination you will be creating a gateway. The gateway is through your spiritual self. Imagine allowing your spiritual self to inter the realm of all that is. You see, there is a frequency, an energy that has all the connections to forever. Nothing is lost. All you have to do is allow. To allow is to let go and release. Let go of all that your brain knows. Your brain is limited. Allow a free flow. Imagine energy waves freely flowing through you.

The truth is that you are a part of forever and you will always be connected to all that is. Your Truth. Therefore, believe in yourself. No matter what others say or do, believe in yourself. You are made from infinite love. You will always be a part of infinite love. When in question go inside. That is where the answers are. We suggest you come to know the deeper levels of truth that you hold and have access. Practice going past your brain and the brains of others. Practice going into your inner truth. The easiest way is to relax into nothingness- which means out of your brain. Practice.

OUR MESSAGE, YOUR TURN

We want you and everyone to know about the beginnings and ends. It is time for the people of Earth to know that NOW is a beginning of a new way for earth. The Now Books are written so that everyone can understand the true meaning of your existence, and your direction while in body. These books are direct words from the Teachers. We, the Teachers have experienced embodiment and we understand the ways of physical people. It is our desire to bring you back on track- back to a world of love. Our words are for everyone. One planet, one source of love. You are the ones who can create the change into peace. We can guide but the change is up to each individual. Now is your turn.

THE VIEW FROM NOW

PART TWO

In this final section we will discuss your answers to world peace. Once again we say that world peace will not come from world leaders. Don't look to them for the answers. World peace will come from the change in each individual. If it is peace that you want, then go in peace. If it is death through suffering that you want, then create suffering through living in negative energy. We have been teaching these messages for thousands of years. It is time to listen and act with peace. Your time is now. The messages are simple. Believe in your power of love. Believe in HEF, high energy frequency.

PRACTICE LOVE

It is time to focus on love, the highest frequency available. It is through this pure energy that earth will be saved. It is through joy, and happiness that the energy of earth will change. We think that the words joy, happiness, and love have been overused without creating positive energy. You know the words, we know the energy that the acts of joy, happiness, and love create. For you to see the words but not act on them is not changing the world. The words are about creating a vibration. The vibration comes from your heart area. The vibration creates laughter, and smiles. We ask you to create and experience. We ask you to be silly more often. Is that so difficult? We don't think so. We ask you to move away from judgments and blame. They serve no positive purpose. Yes, notice the differences but don't apply a good-bad rating on the differences. Know that you are no better or worse than the other person. You are both in different bodies to have different physical experiences. Enjoy your experience as best you can. Let the other person do the same. That is practicing love. The time to begin is now. Your physical view is now. Let it be now.

THE ONLY WAY OUT OF SUFFERING IS THROUGH LOVE

There is talk about how difficult the physical life can be and how difficult it is to experience high frequency while suffering- while being sick, cold, hungry, poor, or scared. We understand. We have had the experiences and offer these words to help bring people of earth out of these conditions. THE ONLY WAY OUT IS THROUGH LOVE. The way to continue poor conditions is through negative energy. Do you understand this? Everyone is involved. Everyone has the opportunity to expand positive energy frequencies. Those who are suffering can create huge differences by mixing playfulness and joy in with their suffering. If your child has died, remember the smiles you shared. No matter what your situation, imagine and remember a different time. If only for short moments, bring peace to your suffering. If death is eminent, know that the spirit will be returning to love. The spirit will be greeted by other loved ones. If your situation is temporary, visualize the before and the after. Visualize a time of high frequency laughter, playfulness, and love. The only way out of suffering is through love. The only way to change the suffering on planet earth is through love, joy, happiness, smiles, giggles, and dancing.... Practice.

The homeless, the imprisoned, and the hospitalized or institutionalized can be helped with love. Instead of judging, offer moments of peace. Offer kind words. And know that their spirit is made of the same love as your own. It is just a role that everyone is playing. Once you and they return from the physical adventure, the oneness, the sameness will be apparent. Don't wait until you leave your body. Practice non-judgmental kindness and change the frequencies surrounding earth. Now is your time to make a difference. While in physical body, no matter your role, or your situation- make a difference for high frequencies.

Keep in mind that now is your time. This is your opportunity to change the frequencies of planet earth and far into infinite space. It is your turn to create a loving planet. You have the instructions. The instructions are a part of your blueprint, your permanency. Practice beginning NOW. Your opportunity starts with desire then belief.

THE FEAR AND THE LOVE OF PHYSICAL LIFE

We are aware of hesitancy in some people. Like standing with wings on the edge of a cliff, there may be fear and uncertainty. If you love, you may get hurt. If you jump you may fall. True. There are endless possibilities in a love-based future- all of which return eventually to infinite love. NOW is your turn. You can take it or leave it. You can keep cycling between the physical and spiritual world as often as you desire. No one will push you off the cliff to endless love. When you desire love more than the chaos and excitement of physical life, you will choose. We will admit that physical life is an exciting adventure. Try to imagine the adventure with joyfulness. Try to imagine a physical life with happiness, joyfulness, and love. It is a possibility, but only when everyone agrees that everyone is worthwhile. Not only are humans worthwhile but so are plants, animals, and rocks- the dirt that your physical body contributes to. Once you decide to value all that is, you will be contributing to all that is. Until then, you will be contributing to pieces of all that is. We suggest that you expand. View the total and contribute to the all.

We want you to know that physical life can be scary, and you have the ability to make it loving.

YOU ARE ENDLESS LOVE

Today we will talk about time- which is a concept for the physical world but not for the spiritual realm. We think it is good for you to know time is endless. If you think of time as endless, it may bring some relief. You are endless in an endless time. Therefore, all of the people you have loved while in physical form will still be loved in spiritual form. The love does not disappear. We hope this brings relief to those of you who are grieving. Your view from the physical place is of limits. Try to see the bigger picture. Imagine endless love. A physical death does not stop the love. Also, the person who transcended, or in your words died, still feels the love. You see, love is timeless. It has no beginning and no end. The energy of the love you produce will recycle forever. We think that is good to know. We say this to help everyone understand that the love you share will be shared forever. Your shared love is timeless. Centuries from now, or centuries past contain the love that you create in the present. We say, create love. Create as much as you can. Love yourself *and* one another. Feel love every day. Love is not only for giving to another person. Love is a way of being. Everyone has the same opportunity to feel love. It doesn't have to come from another person. You have an endless supply of love from within. Use it. Feel it, see it, touch it, and share it. Now is your time to connect with endless love. Now is your time to create endless love- while you are in physical form. Do not set limits of love. Be generous with love for all. Love the sunrises, the grass, rocks, bugs, animals.... Feel your love inside and share it with the world. Now is your time to create endless love. We want you to know that you are endless love.

KNOW THE GREATNESS

It is time to tell you about greatness; the greatness of life in physical form. As you know, life is a derivative of love. Without the energy of infinite love, there would be no life. We ask that you look at your life as having great importance. We also ask that you live your life with greatness. It is your position, your

100

journey, your purpose to carry forward the creation of love. You do this through the expression of love, joy, happiness and all other high energy frequencies. The more you practice living joyfully, the easier your life will become. Of course the easier your life, the more joyful it will be. Prepare for joy. Make plans to add joy into your day. This is an action. Consciously plan joy in your day. Consciously be grateful for the planned joy in your day. Take time out to express your gratitude. Not because you are being told to do so. Express gratitude because by doing so, more greatness will come. Express again, receive again.

Now, when we speak of living joyfully we mean this to be more than words. We mean this to be an action. Something you do. Everyone. Create joy, look for joy. Look for what matters the most- joy, happiness and love. The search for drama can come to an end. Re-train yourself to look for the best, the greatness, and the fuel of life. We want you to experience the greatness.

HEAVEN AND FOREVERLAND

We are ready to talk about foreverland; commonly called heaven. Does it exist? Yes, but not in the biblical form that most people have come to understand. You see. There isn't a special place in the clouds that holds forever souls. There are no judged persons who get to enter or be denied. Everyone is either in spirit or in physical- in growth or in peace. Isn't that easier to understand? There is no judgment. There is growth, expansion, or peace. Peace is rest. Mostly spirits without body are peaceful. Sometimes wounds of physical experiences are carried forward in spirit after the body is transcended. Yet, always, spirit understands the wounds of physical. That is to say that we in spirit share the emotion of physical. Your spirit in body understands and feels the wounds.

Heaven is a concept. It can mean what you would like for it to mean. Generally, when we speak of heaven, we mean a peaceful place without a physical body. That means anyone can come in and out of "heaven" with desire. And once you practice and get used to it, you can meet up with other loved ones in "heaven" whenever you desire. We hope you will create the desire. What we want you to know is that you are not alone in physical form on planet Earth. All others who have transitioned in and out of body- even you- are still in your loving realm and still available. We realize this may be a difficult concept to belief and to practice. In time, everyone will understand this. For now, let it be known that loved ones are never gone. Also let it be known that you are a loved one to someone and you are not gone either. And so it is in heaven and foreverland.

PLANET EARTH IS ALIGNED WITH PEACE

Now, it is time to introduce a new concept. New to people on Earth is the idea of everlasting peace and love. It isn't a new fact, just a new way of being for people of Earth. You, who have been conditioned to suffer, have not been conditioned to endless peace. Therefore, let us the teachers tell you that everlasting peace is possible and a realistic, reachable way of being. Whenever you are ready to hear, to see, the truth of peace is available for you to experience- always and at any time. Now is a good time to *understand* the concept of peace. Now is also a good time to *experience* the concept of peace. Now, is available to everyone. And now you are in body to create. We invite you to be all of what you are in body to be; Love and all of the HEF (high energy frequency) components. Love, joy, happiness, giggles, gratitude... how many HEF components can you name??? Begin the dance into a peaceful planet. No need to negotiate.

We want you to know that planet Earth is aligned with peace. The energy of earth is such that peace is possible. Thousands of years have unfolded to bring Earth to this place and time. You are in body now for the purpose of opening the energy of Earth for peace. We are pleased. Let the unfolding into peace continue.

YOU ARE THE INSTRUMENT OF CHANGE

We are ready to tell you that the best is yet to come. Of course we are aware of the suffering still happening on Earth yet we hope you will be pleased to know that the end is in sight- at least for us who see the larger picture. Meanwhile, spend more time raising the frequencies. We are pleased that many people are beginning to understand and change habits. The change is what makes the difference. Each generation will see less suffering. Each generation will be teaching more about kindness than about judgments and condemnation. More forgiving and understanding will happen. Institutions will focus on the health, happiness, and betterment of the people they serve. This will be a change from self-serving boardrooms with self interests above the majorities.

We can tell you that the best is coming. Be assured that there will be fussing and battles on the way to a peaceful Earth. There will be resistance and reluctance to let go of greed- even though the letting go will bring peace. Can you visualize this new way of being? Try. Find the vision then move towards it. See the peace and become peaceful. See the negative energy and avoid it. You, the individual will make the difference. You the individual will be the force behind mighty breakdowns of negative leaderships. Believe in your power of love. Live your joy, live the peace, and live the love. That is your job. The energy of earth will change because of you. Be the change. Love is your strength. All else will fall into place.

We want you to know that you are the instrument of change.

NOW IS A GOOD TIME

Now, this minute, this hour, this life time; take a moment right now to lift your frequency of love. Right now, take this opportunity that you have to consciously breathe several times. Relax your shoulders. Guide your mind towards the energy in your heart area. Now release and surrender. Drop your shoulders release and let go. When all else is gone, feel the love within. Practice feeling your love from within. Become consciously aware of feeling the love. This may take some practice. Now is a good time to begin practicing the feeling of love within; the infinite love that everyone has.

It is from this place that kindness happens. It is from this place that the best prayer and meditation is communicated. This is also the place where brilliant ideas and miracles happen. We suggest that you go to this place often. You are also invited to ask questions to us from this place. There are always guides willing and able to answer your questions. We want you to know that now is a good time for tuning in to infinite love.

LOVE IS YOUR ENERGY FOR POWERING CHANGE

Now, it is again time to talk about the realization that you are here for a reason. Again we want to say that the reason is love. You are here to move past sufferings of thousands of years. Your path is to understand infinite love. Every single individual is on the same path. Whether you are at the beginning the middle or the end of the path is of no concern. Everyone will eventually end up understanding and living from infinite love. Can you imagine the peace? Try. Imagine the glow of you and all of Earth while radiating infinite love. Want to be a bright star? Radiate love out into foreverland. It is time for Earth to shine. It is time to let other planets know that Earth is full of love and life. Welcome others from faraway places. Welcome them with the glow of love.

We want you to know that Earth is changing because of the energy of love. Your energy will power the change. If you could see in to the not too distant future, that is what you would see- a glowing planet full of love. That is your purpose, your destination.

YOU HAVE THE POWER AND THE RESOURCES

What would you do if you could? If you had all the power and resources in the world, what would you do? Would you live peacefully or in fear? Would you choose to live from a love based or fear based frequency? These choices are yours and always have been. Now is a good time to think about living peacefully. Everything you need for a joyful, peaceful life is available to you. In order to access the wonderfulness, change your energy- change your thoughts, beliefs and actions. If it is peace that you want, begin to think of peace, not struggle. Believe in yourself living in a peaceful way. Act "as if." Act as if you live in a peaceful world. Begin noticing the peace all around you- then begin noticing the peace within you.

If it is peace that you want, don't dwell on fear or horror. Don't dwell on anger and sadness. We can tell you that you *do* have all the resources for peace, love, happiness, and joy. Those energy frequencies are all around you. Those frequencies are available for you to choose at any time. We suggest you start choosing to live with the energy of peace. We want you to know that you *do* have the power and resources. When you choose to tune in to those frequencies, you will see the magnificence of your life.

THE SOFT COLORS OF PEACE

Would you like to know about colors? We can tell you that color really does have different energies, and color elicits different emotions. We are not saying that some colors are better than others. We are saying that there are differences. The energy which you choose to draw upon also has different colors. All the colors serve a purpose and all colors are helpful. All energy is necessary, yet it is helpful to know the differences and when to use that type of help. The energy of peace is transparent. That is because the energy of peace cannot be contained. It does not have limits or boundaries. Peace comes in different soft hues of light. Peace is the feeling of wispiness, or airiness knowing that there is no suffering. Have you felt it? Can you feel it regularly? Can you see it? Peace is available to everyone, no matter what your situation. If you are going into starvation, find peace. If you are about to be killed, find peace. Yes, this is an action. What are your choices? Enter peace or enter fear. We can say that peace and love feel a lot better. Peace and love will never leave you. It is always available. Your fear will come and go. Let it go. Stop the struggle- enter peace.

We understand the difficulty. We understand that people have been trained through thousands of years to enter fear instead of entering love. Entering fear means hate, battle, judgments, depression, death.... Entering love is where you find the best results. This will sound scary to those who were trained to be fearful yet the energy is higher, clearer, further reaching, more pure. All your advantages are in the power of love. Peace comes from letting go of fear. Peace is an expansion of your energy which is an expansion of awareness. Try it. Practice. Visualize peace. When in need, use the colors of soft translucent hues.

THE THRILL, THE EXCITEMENT, THE RIDE OF BEING IN PHYSICAL

Do you want to know about thrills and excitement? Of course you do; the high spiritual energy with lots of physical energy working at the same time. We too, in spirit world enjoy seeing the excitement in physical lives. As a matter of fact- of truth-excitement is a positive energy. Some excitements lead to creation, while others lead to death. Either way positive energy was involved. Therefore, we encourage more excitement. Our suggestion is to get up, get out and be stimulated. Create a positive stimulation. This is along the energy frequency of being joyful, or playful, with your mind, your body, your thoughts... which leads to beliefs, and your behaviors. You have a body now. It is in a limited time. Don't waste it. Use your body for its purpose of expansion of high frequency energy. The good news is that you too will enjoy the trip. Your purpose is connected with enjoyment. Do you get it? You are not here to suffer, you are here to enjoy. The sooner you begin to reprogram, the more love, abundance, joy, happiness... you will experience. Now is a good time to start living in high frequency. It is a choice. A choice is an action. If only for a moment, let the moments build. Your life is thrilling and exciting. Put the thrills and excitement into action, no matter what your circumstance. Keep in mind that circumstances come and go. Did you get the excitement from them? Wow, I lost my home, my love, my life... my spirit lived through it and got peace, eternal love, joy, and happiness. What a ride! Thank you physical body for the adventure.

And now to show our appreciation- the energy of planet Earth is lifting, life will continue. We in spirit are grateful. Thank you for contributing to your personal excitement and to the expansion of life.
With love,
We the Teachers

PEACE IS A CHOICE
If I tell you that now is a time of peace, what would you think? Would you agree or disagree? It isn't a right or wrong question, yet it is about your perspective. You see, because the energy of peace is all around you, this is a time of peace. It is just a choice.

Since the energy of non-peace is also all around, you might be tuned into seeing the violence or the sadness. This too is just a choice. Both energies are present. The choice is yours as to which you want to see, and experience. Doesn't that sound simple?

Not only do you have the choice of energies to see and experience, but your choice produces more of the same. If you want to eliminate a particular energy around you, pay it no attention. If you want to expand a particular energy around you, pay attention to it. Now, what are you paying attention to? If you want to change the energy surrounding Earth, pay attention to one but not the other. Is this making sense to you? How about an example? If you want to be rich, see richness in you and all around you. Even if you are looking at a grain of sand, see the richness in it. If you want to be rich, don't focus on poor, in you or around you. Even if you see a very poor person, find some richness in him, or share some of yours with him. See what you want to create.

Now can we get to world peace? See peace, give peace. Create peace.
We want you to know that peace is a choice.

GRUMPINESS AS A SYMPTOM OF BLAME
Let's write about bickering; also known as the art of complaining. Bickering is about being grumpy then verbalizing the grumpiness. It isn't necessary. As can be expected, grumpiness comes and goes. We say that grumpiness is because of focus. You see, instead of focusing on self love, the attention is on problems "out there." It is a part of blame. Blame your bad words, or bad actions on bad stuff. Often you don't think you have control over the bad stuff so blame happens. Our suggestion for grumpiness is to recognize it, then change your focus.

We want you to know that grumpiness is a symptom of blame. Blame is a judgment. The best way to get out of blame and judgment is through acceptance. When you find peace in the acceptance, your energy becomes more positive. Practice more acceptance.

NOW IS THE TIME OF ACCEPTANCE

Now, we will talk about the age of acceptance. The time has come to accept each other as a particle of the whole. You are, each of you, a particle of the whole that is. With all your differences and misunderstandings, you are all one of the same. You are all infinite love. The easiest, simplest way to be in physical body is to live from your place of infinite love. You don't have to wait for conditions to be right. Start any time any place with your present condition to live in a peaceful planet. Let it be known that Now is the perfect time for acceptance of each other. Also accept that conditions will change when your energy changes and the energy of earth will change when the people of Earth change. It would be in the best interest of all to create a change towards positive energy.

What we are talking about is to lighten up. Don't be so serious. Become more playful. Be more loving and appreciative of your planet. To those of you who govern- in your home, your community, or your country, do so from the heart- from your connection to infinite love. Know that your constituents are your helpers. Treat them with fairness. What you give to yourself, give to all others.

The time has come to recognize the importance of your actions. Pay attention. Act with kindness- for yourself and for others. These words are overused, yet the message is underused. How many times, how many ways must you hear messages of peace, love, kindness, laughter, joy before you begin to act on those words? A good idea would be to act accordingly every time you hear or see a word from the love end of the spectrum. If you pick up a rock where someone has written the word LOVE, make it an action. Think of it as a reminder and act accordingly. Breathe into your loving self. And the same applies to all other words of kindness towards yourself and others. Act on it in the moment. Each moment changes the energy of Earth. We want you to know that now is the time of acceptance.

YOUR MISSION IS WITH PURPOSE

We appreciate you. If you are in physical form, you are working on a message. Whether the message is on the *good* end or the *bad* end, still you create awareness which creates change for the people of Earth. It was your personal challenge to experience Earth as you did, and to extend the message of your experience for others. And NOW, with this in mind, we can all curve the path of our messages towards peace. For those of you who have been living in troubled, un-loving times, curve towards peace. Give it up. Let go. There is no need to die being the victor of defeat. The reason to die is that you have completed your spiritual mission. Go in peace; go in knowing that your energy benefited the whole. It is with gratitude that we appreciate all of the comings and goings into Earth's physical realm. Each coming and going produces a change- for the self and for the energy of the planet. It is with love that you are received in each realm- the coming and going of spiritual and physical energy. It is with love that the missions will continue until all participants understand peace. With the understanding, their Earth will be peaceful. We welcome the movement to peace. We want you to know that your mission is with purpose, and you are appreciated.

Creating a peaceful planet takes time. Now is your time- no matter what level of your mission, know that you are loved.

110

YOU ARE THE REASON, THE STRENGTH AND THE LOVE OF TOMORROW

Now is your time because NOW is when you are alive on physical earth. Take this to heart. Take it with understanding. YOU ARE HERE FOR A REASON. THE REASON IS TO CREATE EXPANSION THROUGH CHANGE. Each time you enter and exit physical existence, your spirit has changed, grown, enlarged, expanded. Your spirit is energy. It contributes to the energy of earth. Speed it up. Know that you are perfect. You are a perfect breath of energy to complete your mission for all that is. This is not only about your life. It is also about the live of earth and the life of forever. Contribute, and give; use your love, your energy of survival. We are waiting for your contributions. They are desired. It must come from each individual. It must come from you. We want you to know that you are the reason, the strength, and the love of tomorrow. Let it be, Now.

Furthermore, for all the love that we witness on Earth, we thank you. We thank you for the brightness that you create. Continue and multiply your energy of love. Let it be.
With gratitude,
The Teachers

THE CHANGE OF YOUR BELIEFS

There is more to say about change. Now is the time of change. Whatever your beliefs, now is the time to look more closely. You can think of it as spring cleaning for the brain. Some beliefs may need to be modified; other beliefs may need to be discarded. You will know the keeper beliefs because they are the ones that make you happy, peaceful, and loving. Keep the good stuff, and get rid of the stuff that drains your energy.

We feel a "How to" coming on. How to get rid of the parts of me that has always been. Example, I was born and raised to be.... Now is a good time to examine what you were born and raised to believe. Ask yourself a few questions. Do the old beliefs create happiness in me? If not, toss it. How about love in me? Certainly, if you don't feel self love, toss whatever is holding you back. Know that no matter what you were told and taught to believe, you are magnificent. You are glorious. You are a wonderful part of all that is. This physical journey that you are on is not all that is. There is much more to you- your spirit of love. It is time to experience the *all-ness* of your greatness. No matter what your experiences have been, believe in your loving connection to all that is.

Now we imagine hearing, "then why am I suffering, loving, happy, miserable, depressed, joyful.... "The answers are that you are having a spiritual growth adventure. How can your spirit possibly know what all this is if you don't have the experiences? Take it for what it is... an experience that will come and go. Then when you reach all that is, you will know it intimately. That is to say, as your spirit grows through physical experiences, it is getting closer to the love of forever; closer to the love of life and the love of always. At the end, your spirit will be aligned with the greatest energy- the energy of love. It can only arrive having rid itself of greed, judgment, fear, sadness, etc. The only way of getting through these negative experiences is to understand them- to experience the depth of all other energies.

You all will cycle through life experiences many times before reaching the love of forever. Sometimes the pain is too difficult for one physical incarnation. Sometimes the same lesson will come several times. In the end, all lessons will be learned. All spirit energy will be of love energy. Take your time. Learn to know that your times of suffering are aspects of the physical brain. When you return each time to spirit, there will be relief- a time of respite. Know that you are not doomed to negative energy. Know that you are doomed to loving energy. In your knowing, go in peace wherever this incarnation is taking you. Go in peace knowing that this too will change. You are loved. You are love on a mission. Don't let the physical experiences and beliefs become overwhelming. Take them as they are; a short time in lessons of understanding that you are the love of forever.

YOUR PATH TO LOVE

And now, we can say that you have a "how to" book of life. The answer of how to live the best life is to live joyfully. DO NOT LIVE DUTIFULLY.   And do not judge those who are living differently. Live your life, learn your lessons, knowing that everyone is doing the same. Whenever you can, help out the ones who are down. Give them a hand up. They will learn the lesson of being down and helped. They will learn the lesson of love. There spirit will understand even if the physical body does not. Give, and receive the lessons of love. That is all you need to do. Give and receive the lessons of love. Remember that in this incarnation you may be on the bottom or the top of the social list. Remember that it is not about your social status, it is about your love status. How many incarnations will it take for you to get it? Get the best you can with this incarnation. Learn the lessons of love. Learn not because I say to. Learn because it will save you a lot of time- incarnations. Either way, the path is the same. Love is where you will arrive-The high energy frequency of love of life.

PEACE COMES THROUGH BREAKING THE CONFINEMENTS

It is a good time to write about imprisonment. Mostly, the prisons we will talk about are those of mind. Those the brain generated. What a waste. Prisons of the mind, the country- the prisoner of wars, or of crimes are all similar. You see, all prisoners you included, lack the freedom of exploration and the freedom of expansion. The glass ceilings and the brick walls have the same effect of limiting freedom of positive energy expansion. Pay attention. Come to understand the boundaries that you put into place. Pay attention to the limits of personal expansion of positive energy. We understand that prisons are necessary for times of separation. We also realize that separation creates a division from growth. That is to say, separation eclipses the view.

The view of the whole is important for positive growth. It is with understanding that you are a larger part of the whole, of all that is, that your growth will develop. When the prisoner, of the physical or of the mind is freed, it is then that expansion can happen. We ask that all guards and guarded recognize the limitations they set on the progress of expansion of love on Earth. Wake up. Realize that your attempts to guard are also restrictive. Whether the guarding comes from within or comes externally, wake up and recognize it. If you are a guard, you are limiting the free flow of loving expansion. Take some time to consider this. Allow the retraining of the guardian and the guarded. Allow the flow of love with the components of peace, joy, and happiness to break through the walls of prisons. It is the only hope, the only success, the only way. Break through to peace for all. Retrain the heart to welcome inner love. Begin with exploring internally. Go inside yourself, to your place of heart, of love. Experience the peace. Let it be. All will follow naturally. We want you to know that peace comes through breaking the confinements of entrapped fear- for both the guard and the guarded.

TRANSCEND AND BE FREE

We will speak more about entrapment- the walls both physical and imagined. In reality, there are no walls of entrapment- not physical or mental. That is because your spirit can and will transcend any wall if it should desire. Your spirit *can* avoid entrapment. There are times when your spirit chooses to stay within confines, for a while, for a lesson- a feeling. Then the spirit will leave. It always happens and it always will. Let it be known that your suffering in confinement is limited because of infinite love. Come to know and understand this infinite power of love within you. If you want the easy life, which most of you do, then live from the power of love, joy, peace, and happiness. You see, the high energy frequency of love doesn't have resistance. It is resistance that creates the difficult life- the stress, and the struggle. Doesn't that make sense? The less resistance you experience, the easier life will be. For the times that you do experience resistance, give up the fight as soon as you can. The longer you stay with low energy, fear, anger, sadness... the more difficult life will be. We understand that events will happen that you don't like. We are saying to spend as little time as you can with your negative energy and misery of the event. Get back to high frequency quickly. Even if you go in and out of high frequency during your time of misery, it will help.

We are telling you that no matter what happens while you are in a physical body, life will be easier when you are tuned into the high frequency of infinite love. Regularly, daily, breathe in to the feeling of love, joy, happiness. Make it a habit. Eventually and with practice, feeling and experiencing this high frequency will become easier and so will your life, and your experiences. What we want you to know is that you have the power to live an easy life.

YOU ARE EXPANDING IN LOVE

Let's continue with the theme of love and how to make it a part of your life. Do you practice meditation? Meditation is a good time to draw into your awareness, the energy of infinite love. When we say love, we also mean to include the other high energy frequencies. Any smile, grin, joy, or happiness is a good energy. When you sit in meditation, you are sitting in stillness, and quietness. This is a perfect time to practice tuning into infinite love. Meditation offers the space to get quiet, get calm, go to your breath, and relax into infinite love. It's a wonderful experience, and a perfect practice field for the big games. The big games are the life events. Life events are best performed with infinite love. The pleasant and unpleasantness of life is made easier through your practice of connecting with infinite love. As we have said, you weren't meant to be alone on this physical adventure. Your spiritual guides and friends are a part of your connection to the network of all that is- to love. Take advantage of this offering. It is always available. You are never alone or away from love.

And now, take a moment to breath into your love within. Be quiet, be still, and notice the inhale and exhale of your breath. You *are* love. You are a piece of all that is- love, life. No matter where you are in your spiritual journey, you are and always will be connected to the love of forever. You *are the love of forever*. Breathe in to the knowing. We want you to know that you are here for a limited time and each incarnation brings you closer to experiencing the full range of energy frequencies. You are expanding in love. Let it be.

YOU ARE THE LIGHT, PRACTICE THE SHINE

Now, we will talk about the wonderfulness. It is time for YOU to experience the greatness, the joy, the amazement that is yours. In this physical life, rejoice in the adventures that will grow your spirit towards everlasting life. Yes, ever-lasting. You have probably heard these words before but didn't take them meaningfully. We would like to apply meaning. It is not about what is waiting for you after death. It is about what you are building in this life time- and however many more life times it will take for you to reach the end of struggle. We can say that struggle will end when you allow. That does not mean the events that cause struggle will end in your current incarnation. It means that you will not see the events as struggle. That day can come. With readiness, you will be able to see with a different lens. The filters will change. The murk will become clear. As you get closer, the waves will become ripples. The ripples will become still waters.

Now. How can you speed the process? How can you find direction? How many life times will it take? The answer- when will you begin living in H.E.F. When will you give up the struggle and begin living in High Energy Frequencies. When will you live in infinite love?

Start with yourself. Start by connecting to your own self love. Once that door is opened, the other doors will begin to open. Start with yourself. You are the center of your universe. All of your love expands from you. In time, you will see the events in your physical life as being just that- events. Your peace will come not from leveling the events but from rising above them- rise above by transcending. This comes with the practice of living in HEF; high energy frequencies of infinite love, joy, abundance, happiness, giggle-ness. Know that you are the light of forever. Practice the shine.

ON THE PATH TO JOY

Now is a good time to think about completion- completing the mission of joy. As we have said, first, you have to believe it is possible. Let me ask you again. Do you think it is possible for you to live joyfully, and lovingly, more often than not? No matter what your life is like right now, can you see a possible path to joy? You may not be on the path, but can you imagine its existence? Can you also believe that the energy frequencies of joy are around you and available? If you can imagine and believe this truth, you are on the path to peace.

Now, once in belief of your power to have joy and peace, align with the frequency. If you believe it is possible, open your heart to feel joy. It can be done, any time, any where. Wherever you are right now, open to peace and joy. Breathe in to your chest, your heart area, and feel. Adjust what you feel until you reach a positive feeling. Stay as long as you can with that positive feeling. Return to it often throughout your day. Understand that by doing this experiment, you are practicing living in the highest energy frequencies. Continue to practice daily. Make a point of practicing in all circumstances. Then give gratitude. As you do this, watch for the goodness, the joy, the peace that comes your way. Enjoy!

INFINITE LOVE IS SEPARATE FROM YOUR EXPERIENCES

We are beginning to see the changes in the people of Earth. We are aware that the movement is in progress. Now is a good time for the movement to gain momentum. It is a good time to pick up speed. You see, what we are asking is for each of you to live a more happy life. The energy of Earth will not get better until people make the change. Once people start living peacefully, joyfully, from their place of love, the energy of Earth will shift. With the shift will be more wellness, and more prosperity and abundance, with less tragedy and suffering. Change the energy, change the results.

Start the process internally. Each person is responsible for the outcomes of the energy they put out. Make this easy. It is much easier to live in peace, joy, and love than it is to live in poverty, illnesses, and drama. Live it up! Make the effort to turn your bad days into good days. It is a choice. YOUR CHOICE. This is about you, not about your circumstances. We want you to know that infinite love is separate from your experiences. Living from the place of infinite love is your choice. Your choices will determine your experiences. Our suggestion is that you smile a lot- from your heart. Keep the momentum going.

THE MESSAGES

We want you to understand Jeshua and Jesus and Lauren. There was a physical man born in flesh. Ho had a spirit within. Just like you. There was an energy source which was more developed than people on earth. This energy source talked through, was a part of, and entered into (most of the time) the physical man. The energy was from a place more than Earth when the man walked the planet. The energy form was more advanced in understanding of the whole of all that is. The energy was a form of what people call love. Or you can call it the energy of life. Or you can call it god- or source. Anyway, the physical form- the man- attracted this energy, and then delivered messages relating to this energy. The messages were not well received by the structures of current rule. Current rule was for the empowerment of the elite, not for the mass. It was decided by the elite in power, to end the messages from the man by ending the man's physical self. But the messages didn't end. They just transformed into other messages which weren't from the developed energy source. The messages were then created to represent the minds of other men of empowerment. Eventually the original messages from the energy form of love- of life were diminished and now almost unrecognizable. It is time to return to the original messages. The messages that serve all of planet earth, not the elite at the expense of the masses. Everyone is a particle of love. Everyone is infinite love and infinite life.

Everyone will eventually become whole again with infinite love. Keep in mind that when we say infinite love, we are talking about a power, a frequency. This frequency is a power above all others. It is the power of life. It is the power of existence. Without it, there would be no life, no advancement, no growth, no expansion. The energy of life, of survival was introduced on planet earth through an energy force. You can say that a bolt of lightning struck a person, and delivered a message, which others tried to extinguish. That isn't a truth, but it is a concept that may help with understanding. DO NOT TRY TO MAKE IT A FACT. The point is that a man was developed further than most men of the time. That made him more open and accessible to further truths. For the record, many other persons throughout time have also been open and accessible and have received messages.

Each of you can be more open and accessible to further truths. Willingness is required. Be willing to believe from within. That means to listen to the voices within. They always speak. They always guide. Listen to the voices which are connected to infinite love. Jesus, and Jeshua, and Lauren (by name in this incarnation) listen from within. You can too. By any name... you are a developed energy source and you have access to the true messages of life. You are so let it be.

JESUS, JESHUA, LAUREN, AND YOU ARE NEVER ALONE

We will continue with who is delivering the messages both in spirit form and in physical form. It is clear that people understand Jesus was/is an enlightened form. There are many others who are enlightened. Jesus was the son of his physical parents. He was enlightened by the energy of love, god, source, the whole... Whatever name you want to apply. He was able to experience the truths and to understand their source and purpose. He understood a life for Earth that would be far more peaceful. His purpose was to present these understandings.

Now, it is time to try again. It is time for the people to hear and understand the messages of peace. His words are in The Now Series Books. They will also continue talking through Lauren and through others. Pay attention this time. Jesus is not the only teacher sharing messages in the books. All the messages are from enlightened teachers. They share the words so that people of Earth will learn of the power that comes from within.

Jeshua was a contributor to Jesus. Jeshua has also walked in physical form on Earth. At the time of Jesus, Jeshua was a helper. Similar to a spiritual guide, Jeshua helped Jesus through the physical existence. They could be considered to be one in the same even though they were in different physical bodies at different times. Still, their mission was the same and they were both enlightened. They helped each other to deliver the message. When Jesus was on the cross, Jeshua was with him in spiritual form, to help through the suffering. Both Jesus and Jeshua are messengers of love, joy, and peace. Jesus did not deliver his message alone. He had helpers. Just as you all have. The same is true for Jeshua. They both had helpers as does everyone.

Your best action might be to learn- to try tuning in to those who are in spirit. They are here to make life easier for you, for earth, for all that is. In your times of darkness and your times of light, tune in from the voices in your heart. Maybe you see them, maybe you hear them, maybe you get the feeling from them. In whatever way you can, receive their support. We want you to know that Jesus, Jeshua, Lauren and YOU are never, were never alone.

LIKE JESHUA AND JESUS, YOU ARE NEVER ALONE
Would you like to know more about your connection to the best, the highest frequency to peace? If so, know that you are it. You are a part of the best that is. That is to say that all energy

frequencies are in and around you. Tune in to the ones of your choice. Just know that when you choose to be angry or depressed- in LEF, (low energy frequency) you can exit whenever you choose. Actually, while you are in LEF for whatever reason, how about looking at it as would an outsider? As we do. Instead of seeing your experience as a drama, see it as a comedy. See it from outside of the situation.

Know that you must have situations which you don't like. It is for growth that you can experience the differences between light and dark, good and bad, wanted not wanted. Whenever you can, don't linger in the not wanted. Shift quickly to the desired. When your physical body, or the body of a loved one is in suffering, shift quickly to the support of your helpers. That may seem like going into a trance state- a non-feeling state. Let it be. Allow you helpers to share the burden. They are always present. Always willing. Always available. Just like Jeshua and Jesus, and all of their helpers, you are never alone.

THE VIEW FROM NOW IS AS PRETTY AS YOU MAKE IT

Now it is time that you know about the best to come. You see, the best is not about having a good day, or a good experience, it is about having a good life and a good eternity. You all have foreverness. Want to make it the best? Of course you do. Tune in to the possibility. Your physical life is for the experience of all the energies. It is in physical form that you come to know all the frequencies. I think you are beginning to understand this. Now, understand that you have choices as to how long you must stay in each frequency. Know that you can accept death, suffering, depression, poverty, as long or as short as you desire. Yes, these are necessary experiences because you chose to enter physical life at this time. And yes, you have the choice to come and go through them all with your own speed. That can mean where ever you are, so is love. If you are in prison, so is love. Go in to quiet or trance. Find your helpers. Find love. If you are in poverty, know that it can be temporary because there is always enough. Take your share. Give some to others. Plant a communal garden. Plant a garden of peace, of love, of prosperity of sharing.

The world will change. Earth will adjust. People will realize that everyone has. No one in physical form is special or above the others. Play your roles and learn your experiences knowing that you are amongst the best. You are amongst the love of forever. That is a truth to live by. We thank you for your time and service for delivering the messages of love. We want you to know that The View From Now is as pretty as you make it.

A MEDITATION OF LOVE, BEAUTY, AND GREATNESS
Can you imagine the beauty of earth once everyone is aligned with peace? Try. Now is the time and the place to view a peaceful loving world. We say NOW because this is where you are right now- in body, on Earth. You are the creators and the vision makers. We are encouraging you to create the vision of a peaceful loving planet. It is with our loving support that we encourage you to live your best and to live from your greatness. Your best and your greatness are connected to the energy of love.

Let's take a moment to form a vision. With eyes closed, view yourself on your planet surrounded by peace, joy, love, and beauty. Take a few moments. See it, feel it, and experience your greatness. Allow your greatness to spill over into the atmosphere. See it as a transparent tranquil form. From your love within, expand your love to your planet. There is enough love within to expand across all of earth and beyond. Take a deep breath and release love. Now, think about making this a habit. Regularly, tune in to your love within and send it out across you planet. Thank you. We are grateful.

THE TRUTH OF YOUR DESTINY

Now is a good time to consider your destiny. While you are at it, consider the destiny of Earth. Who is in charge of the destiny of you and of Earth? If you say "them" can you identify "them"? Can you call them by name or of affiliation- political leader, religious leader, company boss? We will suggest that YOU are the leader of the destiny of you and Earth. It is your energy that is creating change. You are the one responsible for your creation and your contribution to yourself and your planet. Take responsibility. Own it. Acknowledge your power even though you don't see it. Be that which you want the world to be. We will confirm that you are the power. YOU are the change. You are the creator. It is not, and has never been about "them." Even when "them" took control, take responsibility for being a follower. If you want to follow, then follow your love within. Follow your love and truth from your heart. Question "their" statements. Believe in your own truths from within. Your own truths from within are connected to the love of all that is. There are many stories yet only one truth. Connect to it.

With infinite love,

The Teachers

LET YOUR LOVE SHOW UP IN THE WORLD

It is with love that we approach you with our messages. It is our desire to see a loving planet Earth. You have come closer than ever. The energy is shifting to greatness. As you look at the people and struggles on Earth it may be difficult to see the positive energy. We can tell you that it is more brilliant than it has ever been. You who experience the light and love, the joy and happiness, along with the silliness and giggles are in the company of many others. Now is probably a good time to start reaching out to others from your place of love and happiness- from your heart.

Listen inside. If you can't hear, then feel or see the love within. Experience your love. More and more people are experiencing and expanding from a place of love. If possible, connect with these people and strengthen together. Also, smile on those in need. Those who are in LEF, need your loving support. Offer kindness to the homeless, the angry, and the sad. That is what is meant by the saying, "Turn the other cheek." Turn kindness towards those in need. Seek togetherness with others who are already in the light of love. Now is a good time to let your love show up in the world. We want you to know that you are here for the job. Make the best of it.

THINK PEACE, THINK BIG, THINK REALITY

The perfect time to visualize a more perfect world is now. We are talking about a more perfectly peaceful world. Like the perfect worlds in peaceful fairytales. You can build a real life fairytale; a place that you would dream about. Let's start with a dream. In your fairytale, you are the star. You are the one who makes dreams come true. You are the dreamer of a perfect time and place. Can you visualize it? If so, stay with the vision for a while. Does your vision have lush green plants with lovely colors? Does everyone live happily in a home with plenty to eat? Are the people in your vision kind to themselves and to one another? We can imagine your vision, and we can also see the result. You see, what is necessary for this fairytale picture to become a reality, is desire. You can start building your reality right where you are. Right now, notice something that is likeable- a tree, a flower, a pebble, rock or mountain, a smile.... Your dream has begun. Your reality is being created from your vision, your desire, and your belief. More often than not, this will become your experience. When many more people share a similar vision, Earth will become the peaceful dream- the peaceful reality.

You are the dream maker; you are the creator of a reality fantasy world. You have the power to create a *paradise* on your planet earth. It has to start somewhere. Let it start with you. We want you to think *peace*. Think big, think reality.

We think it may be helpful to THINK in groups. While you can create in thought on your own, it is still helpful to add more energy into the thought. Seek out other like-minded people. Earth is scattered with peace-seeking people. Join in. Reach across the continents to join with the unity of a loving earth. The system is set up and in place. The players are getting ready. Now is the time for the game of love, of life, of peace on earth. Join your teammates. Extend a welcome to visit and to share a common goal.

Now is when you have the opportunity to connect with others on the mission of peace, and equality. Don't waste your limited time in physical form. Open to the greater you and share openly. The greater outcome is love for all. We want you to know that it will take all of you to create this reality. Some people have begun, others will start soon, and some will start when readiness happens. Let it be. Don't push. Just be. Be in your state of loving peace. Nothing else is required.

THE WHEELS ARE TURNING TOWARDS PEACE
Know that all is in progress. The wheels of peace are turning. We are grateful. We are thankful for these moments of striving into peace. For all of the participants thus far, we thank you. For every moment that you felt love from within, peace from within and joy from within. We thank you. For every giggle, every smile, every silly dance, we thank you. Give it up. Let go of fear, and negative energy. Let go of the low frequency energies. (LEF) They aren't important for survival or thrive-able for you or earth. Release, let go. Use the energy that is necessary for survival. Use

love, joy, happiness, peace, giggles.... We aren't asking for the fun of it. We are asking for the purpose of it. The purpose is to expand your planet. It can only expand with the energy of love-the high frequencies. It can only expand with your participation.

There is a choice involved here. Extinguish life and earth or expand life and earth. Your choice. You are in body. You have the power. Our choice would be to live happily, lovingly, joyfully, and peacefully. It isn't about us. It is about you. Today. Now. Go ahead, crack a smile. We want you to know that the wheels are turning towards peace. We invite you to jump on board.

IMAGINE YOUR JOY

We will talk about speed. How fast can you imagine? Usually, imagination doesn't take time. It is always available. Now the timely part is the subject of your imagination. If you are imagining despair, then you are probably living in despair. Want a different existence? Change that which you imagine. How quickly can you invent a new picture to imagine? If you are changing your image from despair to joy, do you feel a struggle going on? If so, you can have a conversation with that struggle. Become aware of the struggle and pay it attention. The attention to pay is about holding on to something you don't want. Have you been programmed to believe that you must keep a struggle, keep despair and that you can't see a way out? Were you even conscious of clinging to despair?

You have a choice. No matter what your situation, you can choose to imagine joy. Give yourself a break. Imagine spurts of joy. You have the time and it doesn't take long to do, yet the results can last forever. Bring awareness to your desire. Imagine what you want to be. That is your way out. Start with imagining. We want you to know that timing is important and it is always the right time to imagine joy. Creating your joy will take a little bit of time with a bit of imagination.

YOUR ARE THE SAVIOR

Now, let it be known that you are what matters. You are the beginning, the end, and all in between. The reason for this is that you are the energy of love in physical form. You have the ability to create that which we all wish to have created. You see, we in spirit do not have the creative power because we don't have the physical mass. We are saying to you that now is your time to do the work of creating a loving planet. You will be able to do this through your connection to the source of infinite love. Stop wondering how, and stop procrastinating. Start now by being quiet, breathe, and feel the energy in the area of your heart. Bring your awareness to the high frequency of love. It is there. Believe and become aware.

Know the truths. Most people intuitively know the difference between right and wrong, good and bad, love and fear, positive energy and negative energy. Most people intuitively know which energies help mankind and which energies destroy mankind. All that is needed is to pay attention- to become aware of the energies you are using. The intuitive connection is your lifeline to infinite love, to god, to the whole, the source.... Become aware of your connection and take advantage of it. Act from your place of love and caring.

We want you to know that you are the saviors of yourself, each other, and your planet. YOU are the savior. The Teachers and your guides are here to help but it is your energy that will create a difference.

THE POWER IN FREE WILL

Now let us talk about the differences between naturally occurring events and your free will to choose occurrences. Let us start by saying that you can and do draw to you according to the energy that you emit. It is the energy that you send, radiate, believe in, which becomes the object or occurrence that comes back to you. It can be no other way. You see, that which comes to you was made by you, through your imagination, thoughts, beliefs, or actions. Think of yourself as the controller at the switchboard. You create the flow that comes and goes to and from you. Now, how much free will do you have over this flow? Some things will come to you that you didn't consciously or knowingly ask for. You probably didn't ask for a natural disaster to demolish you home. But you probably did choose, for any of many reasons to have your house in that location which would be in the path of a disaster. Your free will chose the house and its location. The disaster was due to naturally occurring events that you could not foresee.

What we want you to know is that you do have some control over naturally occurring events. The control comes from your free will to choose the energy of earth. Choosing the energy that you want and the abundance, health, relationships, etcetera that you want is the same process as choosing the energy of earth. You can be peaceful and so can earth, if that is the energy you choose. We agree this will take time. To change the energy of Earth, it will take the energy of many participants all wanting peace.

The energy of earth is affected by all the energies which live there. You are that powerful. The sooner everyone begins to live in peace; the sooner peace will be experienced for Earth and everyone. Now is a good time to start. Free will- amazingly powerful!

MORE ABOUT YOUR FREE WILL

We are going to break this down for you again. To start with, there is no master controller out there. No one is creating your life for you. The energy that you choose is what you get. Energy does not have a mind of its own. The energy of love is the most powerful, and most efficient. The energy of love makes life a lot easier. For that matter, the energy of love *is* the energy of life. It is not blaming, discerning, judgmental, selective... it is pure. Nothing in the world of energy has the power to manipulate you. The opposite is true. You have the power to manipulate the energy that comes to you. All things are made of energy.

Now, you may ask, "why don't I have what I want, or why do I have what I don't want." The answer is pure and simple- Be aware, be conscious, of the energy you use. A concern is that you can't always have awareness. True. There is movement in the unconscious. There are experiences that the spirit is in body to learn. Before birth, the spirit (unconscious to most people) was aware of suffering and joy to be experienced while in physical form. It is a choice- free will, to experience all the energies; to know of all before becoming one with the energy of love.

Now, as we have said before, you don't have to become stuck in any particular energy. If you are uncomfortable- sad, depressed, angry... you have a choice, a free will to move out of that experience. This is done by changing your frequency. If you are living in poverty, you can at any time, refuse to remain. Change your frequency to abundance. Live as if you have it all. The energy will begin to follow. At all times, take notice of the change and be grateful. Say your thanks. That too is an energy.

Before moving on we will say that much of the "stuckness," is resistance to change; resistance to getting out of your misery, and resistance to seeing past your situation. Work on it. No one *out there* is controlling you. No one *out there* put your home in a danger zone. No one *out there* can get you back to peace. Your guides will help if you let them. It is your free will.

YOU ARE IN CONTROL

Living from your inner truth and infinite love will provide all the answers you need. Whatever question, or problem you want to solve, the answers can be found within. You may need help learning how to listen from within. We suggest that you practice. Be open and available, and know that the answers may not be in your brain. Allow a movement or a sound to stir within. Don't try to force it. A good time to become aware is early morning before your brain has started chattering, and late night when your brain has stopped chattering. With more practice you may be able to listen within at any time of day and in any circumstance.

Everything in your current life can be answered from within. We are aware of the times of overwhelm because of physical conditions. We are aware of limitations which create a lack... of love, food, health, and money. Some of this leads to violence, anger, or depression. What we are saying is that there is always enough of what is needed. If you feel as if you are losing at playing the physical game of life, then seek from within. Outside of physical awareness there are answers. Your guides are available to help and so is your connection to infinite love. You may know infinite love as god, source, or any other name; we know it as the highest energy frequency. We didn't name it, yet we know it.

We want you to know that you are in control. As a physical being, you will have the ability to experience the dark and the light, the high frequencies and the low frequencies. Still, it is up to you as to how to maneuver through the highs and lows. When you feel stuck, or in doubt, or unknowing, get quiet, breathe, ask within, then act according to your truth. Practice

UNDERSTANDING SUFFERING

We will explain further about suffering; which part is necessary and which part is not. Suffering is always brought on by you. Before you, or shall we say your spirit, entered physical life there was awareness of both positive and negative energy in the physical realm. Your spirit made a decision, knowing that times would be good and bad. There are reasons your spirit chose to re-enter. For whatever specific reason, the overall concern was expansion of positive energy; becoming closer to pure loving energy. The way to do that is to experience all the energies. It is important to have the experiences, not to just hear about them. This takes many life times, depending on the individual spirit. Let it be known that a GOD is not punishing you.

When re-entering, the physical realm, there are roles to be in and experiences to have. Sometimes you may be the murder, sometimes the victim; Sometimes the leader, sometimes the follower or the rich or the poor. All of you can learn from those around you. If your child is murdered, you will learn that pain. If your son is a murderer you will learn that pain. It is easiest to learn without judgment and blame. It may take several incarnations to stop blaming or stop being the victim and accept the tragedy of the experience. Your word is to understand forgiveness. The point is to move on towards love without holding on to the story. When you move on, you are finished with that experience. New births, will have new experiences until the time comes when the spirit will mostly feel positive energy in a life cycle. That will happen when you stop clinging to the pain- the negative energy. That will happen when you can witness and experience without judgment. That will happen when you can let go of someone or something and hold on to the love that was there, instead of holding on to the suffering from the loss. We aren't saying to not experience a negative impact; we are saying don't hold on to it. We are saying to grow in love, not in hate.

You can make your physical experience on earth a lot easier. Let go of what is not serving you. Love and all the positive energies are serving you. Fear and the negative energies are draining you. As your energy is drained, so is your physical health- a reminder that love supports life, negative energy depletes life. We want you to know that you chose to re-enter physical life for the purpose of expanding the energy of love- for yourself and for your planet. Let it be.

THE REASON FOR THANKS AND GRATITUDE

Abundance- drawing to you that which you desire. You want money for a better life. You want the ability to pay bills, to feed the family, and have shelter with a few luxuries. You want to afford medical care and maybe a get-out-of-jail-free-card. The jail or prison is for getting caught while trying to get enough to survive or to thrive. We can tell you that it is all available at your calling. Play by the infinite rules, not the limiting rules of the physical world. The key to having all you need or want is to expect it. Begin now to look at all you have had, and then give thanks. We know you have had because you are still alive. You are still being cared for. You are still drawing to you. Start appreciating instead of denying. Start seeing the all of what has come to you, even if it was in small portions. See it and give thanks. Where ever it came from and whoever has provided, for some reason you are still alive and have been cared for- at least a little bit. Are you thankful? If so, say so. Are you NOT thankful, but revengeful or depressed? If so acknowledge. Do you expect to be given to because you desire? If so, then desire more of what you have had. Give thanks so that more can come. Be grateful for your existence thus far.

What we are saying is to stop whining about not having enough and begin to live with thankfulness for what you have had. Now expand. Expand with the knowing that there is no limit of what you can have. You, yourself, set a limit by regretting what you have had- your lack. When you set a limit with regret, the energy you send is that of *no more*. Therefore what you get in return is *no more*. We suggest that instead, you send the energy of thanks, of joy, of happiness for what you have had and will have. Pay attention and watch for the return. When we say to express gratitude and thankfulness, we say you will be receiving more of the same. The energy you put out is equal to the energy that is returned. Are you getting this now? The reason for gratitude is not because we say so. The reason is in your energy.

PRAISE YOURSELF AND CELEBRATE

We think you are beginning to understand your importance and your power. All along, it was you, each of you who held the power. If you want to give thanks, then include yourself. Be sure to praise yourself for getting you along the physical path towards love. Praise yourself for getting through the rough times. We do. We celebrate you. It would be a wonderful thing to congratulate yourself and others for navigating the physical world. For all your struggles, recognize your greatness. We suggest that you have a greatness celebration party. Now is always a good time to laugh, dance, love, grin, and celebrate. Create merriment by celebrating YOU. Not only is it a fun thing to do, but celebration of self- and others sends a lot of positive energy into the world. Celebrations light up your planet. We are telling you to have awareness and take the action, of enjoyment.

Now is your time. Bring out all the goodness and fun that you can. We want you to know that you have the power and the control. You are the one in charge.

A PRAYER- YOU ARE PERFECT

If only for a while, if only for a little bit open yourself to love. Experience all the joy that you can find. Seek intentionally for the best there is. If we said a prayer for you, this would be it. We would pray for your love, your joy, happiness and peace. We see that the energy is available to you all. We pray you will find it. It is with love that we offer ourselves to you. We offer to walk with you, to laugh with you, and to cry with you because we care deeply for you. We understand your job in the physical realm because we too have walked on Earth. We are here to be of service to you. Even though most of you can't see us, we are here. Even though most of you can't hear us, we talk to you. Keep talking to us because we always listen. We can't physically hold you to share our love, but we do in spirit.

We appreciate you and we are grateful for the work you are doing. Each and everyone, no matter your circumstances, we love you and we appreciate you. Know that you are not judged from the spiritual realm. We know that you are all learning, you are all experiencing, and even though you can't always see it, you are all moving closer towards the love of the whole of all that is.

As you travel through positive and negative energy, know that we travel with you. The experiences are yours. We can't save you from them, or choose your experiences for you but we can be with you, share your feelings and love you all the way.

Know that you are perfect because you are a part of all that is. You are a part of infinite love and recycled foreverness.

With love,
The Teachers and Guides

JESUS SAYS, YOU ARE A BEING OF THE TRUTH

I am here and ready to speak. I am the one you call Jesus. It is my purpose to say that you are the important one. You are the ones creating change. My message was and is about you. It was not about me. It is time for you to change the focus from past stories about me, to present stories about YOU. I am not your savior. I am your teacher. It is your turn now. Awaken within you the love of forever. Your love and your foreverness. You are me at a different time. That means the love I carried within me is the same energy of love that you carry within you. It is time for you to stop shifting the importance of you to me. Now is the time for you to do the work of creating a loving planet. Don't look at me, look within yourself. You will become the teachers by becoming the doers. Take responsibility. Live from your truth within. Do not live from what someone else has told you to believe. Your truth is connected to the truth of all that is. *You are a being of the truth.* Listen from your heart, and then carry forward. Is your heart in conflict with your brain? Choose your heart. In all times choose gentleness, kindness, peace, love and joy. By doing so, you will always be listening to your heart.

Let's put this into a perspective of now. If you are told that you will be rewarded for following an authority, does your heart and brain agree or is there conflict, discontent, and uncertainty within. If your heart agrees, then follow. If your heart is in conflict, don't follow. I'm just trying to make it easier on you. There will be no need to clean up a mess if you don't make one. Yet, if you do follow the brain while in conflict with the heart, there will probably be a lesson to learn. You have forever to learn lessons. You will not be judged. You will be loved. Your choice, your free will- as always.

We want you to know that you are loved, not judged, you have forever to explore the paths, and we will always be with you. All paths will eventually lead to the truth of love.

136

THE NEW INTELLEGENCE

Our talk now is on ignorance. It is time to remove the veil of unknowing. There comes a time, and the time is now to view your world through a different way of thinking and being. Now is the time for the view of a loving world- your home. You are the ones who will build this new view. People will be performing according to new rules. Everyone on Earth will be included. The new intelligence will not be self serving or based on greed and power. The new intelligence will create a loving abundant place for all inhabitants. The goal of new intelligence will be to discover ways of co-existing in peace instead of dominance and suppression. The new intelligence will recognize that every life has a purpose, and the new intelligence will honor that purpose.

It is fitting to understand the changes that are in progress. As we have said, many people are already in line with peace and others will be making the shift over the next generations. There will be an accumulative effect as more people become the example and more babies are born into a caring and loving world.

We say for you to begin the vision. Begin to see what a H.E.F. (high energy frequency) loving and peaceful world will look like. Begin to imagine then begin to act. Wake up the ignorant, unknowing, unaware part of you which can be inconsiderate and demeaning. Now is the time to see clearly the view of a loving world. It is possible and it is up to you... and you... and you.

We want you to know that the view from a loving Earth is spectacular. We can see bits and pieces and we anticipate the full showing. Wake up Earth. Remove the veil of ignorance and exchange it for a veil of loving intelligence.

THE MEEK WILL INHERIT

When it was said that the meek will inherit, understand it to mean love will inherit. Love is not forceful; it doesn't use weapons of destruction. Love does not plot and plan ways to kill others and steal their homes, land or sustenance. Love is gentle and kind. The earth will be inherited through the energy of love.

The word meek was not meant to mean submissive and weak, as the connotation may now imply. Meek does not mean weak. It is the gentleness of love that will survive the harshness of negative energy. When you think of an inherited Earth, think of the strength of love outlasting the fear; high energy frequency (HEF) outlasts low energy frequencies (LEF). Love will outlast fear. Love has no limits, therefore love is forever. Fear is limited therefore cannot continue forever.

Now we will talk in terms of high energy frequency and low energy frequency. The terms are more encompassing then the terms of love and fear. The term "meek" has changed over the centuries. It is meant to mean the compassionate, the loving, and the joyful. Where in time did meek begin to mean the weak, the submissive? We can assure you that the high frequencies are far more enduring than the low frequencies. Earth will be inherited by high frequencies or not at all. If low frequencies dominated, Earth would no longer show signs of life.

We want you to know that yes, the meek will inherit. The meek meaning the high energy frequencies of which love is the highest. It is time to put away the weapons of destruction. They won't be needed for the continuation of Earth. Love will prevail or nothing at all.

THE NOW BIBLES

It is with much love that we continue with the writings. In time, the entire world will know of these books. In past days and other languages books were called bibles. In that perspective, we say to you that these are the new bibles, the new books; The Bibles for Life on Earth Now- not then. Things change. Many changes have happened over thousands of years. It is time to get current. For continued life on Earth it is time to accept a fresher perspective. We invite you to accept The Now Bibles. If you want a guide as to the best and easiest way to live life and if you want peace for all of earth then here is your study guide. Here are your reference books. Here is the way to teach your children and generations to come. It gives us great pleasure to re-introduce love to you. The messages have changed over the years, yet the core was always, love is life. Are you beginning to understand? Love- your name for this energy- is the frequency of always. It is your turn to change the frequencies, to see, feel, sense, the energy that you are putting out. For any occurrence, feel its energy, then respond. Over time, over millions of years, as the brain developed, people begin to abandon the connection to life, to love (as we call it). As the brain developed, which is a good thing; people begin to listen from the short cut. The brain was a quick answer for immediate problems. Of course it created a secondary problem. The brain is temporary and not connected to the whole of all that is.

You are connected. It is time to reconnect. Let it be known that love, which means life, which is energy, is your highest connection and your only hope for forever. Forever means peace. It can be no other way. Now is your time. Now is when you will create the connection to forever. Let Earth live now. And so it is.

YOU ARE LIFE BECAUSE LOVE IS LIFE

We are very excited to share with everyone that Now is the time to expand the energy of who you are. You are the energy of forever, of the whole, of all that is. You are Love. You are life because love is life. Love is an energy. It is not a god. You are in control of your expression of love, and you are in control of your ability to feel love. Once again, we are not talking about the love for another person. We are talking about feeling self love in you connection to infinite love. There is a way that you can feel you own love, your self love, unconnected to other life forms. If you are totally alone, you could still feel your loving connection to all that is. Also, you could still feel your connection to your spiritual guides.

We want you to know that yes; loving one another is a positive good thing. We also want you to know that all you need is to love yourself through your connection to all that is. Both loves feel the same, although self love with connection to infinite love is greater- and feels greater. That means, you can love your pet, your spouse, your offspring, your country, yet love of self through connection to infinite self is strongest. In this incarnation- or any incarnation, you never have to lose love if you love through self, and your connection to infinite love. Believe that you are a part of the best. You are a part of life which is a part of love. It can be no other way. Life is the energy of love. Trust it, and experience infinite love. It is what you are made of.

A NEW FREEDOM FROM KNOWING YOUR ENERGY

We are here to talk about your new freedom. We wish for you all to know that a new freedom waits for you all. That is to say that everyone can experience a new way of being and a new lightness about them. Some of you will experience this; others will stay in doubt, therefore outside of the new experience. The new experience is about the glow of peace, love, freedom, joy, happiness, and all the other high frequency feelings. We call this a freedom because it is liberating. Once you experience the separateness from low frequencies, you will feel liberated. Once you learn to live, more often than not, from this new freedom, you will want more. That is to say that once you begin living in the freedom of HEF, it will become your new choice of physical existence. In time, the entire planet will choose to live in HEF. All you have to do is create awareness, then make a decision.

Become aware of your energy. When you wake up in the morning make time to cycle through a few emotions- energies. If you wake up feeling down, become aware, then begin to cycle your emotions, your energy upward. It doesn't matter what bad dream or event got you down. Make a choice to experience a higher energy before you get up to start your day. Practice.

Throughout your day instead of checking your thoughts, check your energy. I'm thinking... about an event in my day. Check my energy, my emotion about the event. End the check with HEF, not LEF. That means to end with a high energy frequency, and not a low energy frequency. Work at it. This may not be natural for you. That is why we are suggesting that you practice awareness, and then make adjustments. In time, this will become automatic; just like it was in the beginning of humanity. Before the struggle for survival lead to different paths, there was an awareness of internal peace. Now is the time to return. This is your time to begin the path towards high energy frequencies on Earth. This is your time to begin saving life on Earth. Pay attention. Notice your thoughts, your beliefs, your behaviors, AND YOUR ENERGY.

We, the Teachers, believe in you. We have faith in you, as you have faith in us and in your spiritual guides. We are all one Love, one Purpose, one Whole.

THIS IS YOUR TIME, THANK YOU FOR PARTICIPATING

This is the time of expansion. This is the time of growth for Earth. Whether you are animal, vegetable or mineral, this is your time. We are sending these words to humans who will affect all of Earth because humans have the greatest capacity of using high energy and low energy. Other parts of earth- animal and mineral mostly use survival without negative energy. We will explain more about this in the next book- The Book of Infinite Love. For now, know that you, as a human can do more relaxing into comfort. There is no longer a need to compete for survival. All of you have all that is necessary, and you have the intellect (the brain) to help you. For other animals and minerals, they too have their purpose. They are here for a reason and they live as you live. Your planet life is more than human life. Be aware and be respectful. To disrespect another part of Earth life is to disrespect the whole of all that is. Stop putting yourself above the whole. You are merely a participant in the whole. So is the roach, the rat, the weed, or any other undesirable. You are not greater or more important in the view of the whole. You are a participant. All of earth participates in its growth and expansion into a universe of life; a universe of freedom and foreverness. Become one with all that is. Make life easier for you and for all. Become one. Breathe a sigh of relief by acknowledging that you are a shining light for the whole.

This is your time. This is why you are here NOW. You made a choice to enter physical life at this time. As either the protagonist of the antagonist, you are here to create awareness. We celebrate you all. We don't judge you differently. We ask that you consider you own personal awareness of your energy. It is a part of your purpose. We love you all. Each of the lessons through incarnation will bring you closer to forever love. Thank you for participating on your path. Thank you for acknowledging your energy on this trip.

THE HOW-TO OF EXPANDING YOUR ENERGY

Now that you are here, let's begin a new journey. We will use you as leadership. You, the people of earth, are the leaders of its survival. Doesn't that make sense to you? The power is in your hands, not in a mysterious disaster-love seeking god. You are the energy of Earth. Step up to the plate. Step up to your role. We can talk to you, and we can hear from the rocks and trees. All of the energy of Earth wants peace. It is the humans who are making the difference. If you are a human and reading this, then you are making a difference.

The difference you make for yourself and Earth is determined by the energy you are using. What kind of difference do you want to make? When you leave your physical body, what condition will Earth be in because of your presence now? This is your chance right now. Make the most of it.

What we are saying is that Earth will expand in positive energy if you create the connection. Earth will expand in negative energy if you create the connection. Your love will expand when you allow the *connection*. When you learn to use your spirit, your heart, your love, you will expand in that direction. You will be the peace when you choose to listen from your spiritual connection; when you listen from the energy in your heart. All you have to do is practice breathing into that area. Leave the brain energy behind for a while, as you learn. Feel, instead of think or know. Sometimes you just need to feel the love within. Once you do, and once it becomes a habit, your life will be easier- and so will the life of Earth. Make it easy on yourself and others. Make it easy on your planet. Breathe into infinite love.

EXPAND INTO HIGHER FREQUENCY

Can we be more direct or less confusing? Can you take a leap of trust and believe in the messages? We are asking for yourself and for your planet, that you expand into positive energy and not negative energy. That is the message. We are asking that you trust and let go of negativity which is fear. We are asking that you embrace love which includes joy, happiness, and peace. Toss some smiles, some giggles, and laughter into your life. Tune into and experience the best that life has to offer. Even when you are down, check your energy. Know where you are and what you are putting out. Know which energy will help you and which energy will harm your spiritual growth. Become aware and activate the best in you. Whatever you are confronting, use the energy of love. It is your easiest escape. Breathe into the love within which is not in your brain. The love within is your guide, and your direction- if you want an easy path. YOU can stop suffering and start being in peace. As always, it is your choice, anytime. Now is a good time.

It really is that simple- make a choice. All else will happen for you. Wherever you are right now on your path, now is the time to choose your best energy. We want you to know that now is always a good time to choose the energy of love. We don't call it love. We feel the energy, but you can call it any name you choose. Expand into higher frequency.

THE GIFT

You are the gift. You in physical form are the gift to your spirit and your planet. The gift of being in embodiment means that the desires of the spirit can be fulfilled. The same is true for the "spirit" of planet Earth. In physical form, you can expand energy. This is your mission, and your purpose. Your call to action is for the expansion of positive energy. To do so, you must live in positive energy. Your experiences must include positive energy.

144

You have to make the change away from negative energy. This is when you get to use your brain which includes your thoughts, awareness, and beliefs- both conscious and unconscious. Think about the energy you put out and what type of energy you want to experience. Gain awareness of your energy and make a choice. Challenge your beliefs. Open up to the belief of an easier life for you and peace for all of Earth. You can do this with practice. As you shift through emotional energy throughout your day, consciously choose to stay longer with the high frequencies. When you are in low frequency, notice with awareness. Make a conscious effort to shift into higher frequencies. This can be done no matter what your reason for being in low frequency. Practice.

Be the gift of love, joy, and happiness.… Make it your gift to yourself and to the world. In peace and gratitude, we thank you.

YOU HAVE ENLIGHTENMENT AND CHOICES

We the teachers are the founders of these new books- The Now Books. We gave you the words for the purpose of enlightenment. The books are to shed a new light so that everyone can understand the ways of peace, through love. Peace is a by-product of infinite love, or as we say, high energy frequency. Everyone has access. No matter your position in life, peace and love are available to you. You are in control. It is up to you to choose the higher energy frequencies of love and life or to choose the lower energy frequencies that will harm or destroy. The information is presented. Humans have intellect and choice. The consequences are worth analyzing and considering.

The future is up to you; your future of personal peace with happiness and the future of life on Earth. We see both paths of love and paths of destruction. Both paths are clear in our vision. The end results will be with you, the path makers. Now is the time to view a path of… we can feel it but we don't find the word.

What would you call a path of... forever? The forever path is... a feeling of wonderfulness.

We want you to know that you have the words and the enlightenment. Now the choice is yours. The entire spiritual and physical world awaits the outcome. How many generations will succeed you?

BECOME ONE WITH YOUR FOREVERNESS

If we, through our words, have instilled movement in you, we hope it will be a movement towards love. We cannot force you, change you, or rule you. We can shine light on the direction of life. It is up to you to stay in the light and follow the easiest path, or divert to any path you choose. No one governs you. Each person has the free flowing energy of life going through them at all times. Each person has the ability to choose the most desirable energy. The short paths of greed, murder, and low energy frequencies will not bring you to your destination of infinite love, satisfaction, peace, pleasure....

We recognize the struggle that some of you have. We recognize the struggle of power and greed. Keep in mind that your lifetime gains of power and money do not carry over to the next life or infinite life-love. Someone needs to be in power. Abundance is always available to everyone. Just know that these traits are good for one lesson in one incarnation. The life time gains in one incarnation will equal the amount of high energy frequencies you have experienced and shared with your planet. In the end, you are headed towards contributing to forever energy. All of life contributes to the same energy, no matter what planet you are on. For now, just hear this. At some point you will understand; maybe in this incarnation or maybe thousands of years from now. Still you are valued for your input. Either way, you can make life easier on yourself and all others whenever you choose to work with the greatest power. You are energy and always will be. You are the energy of love-life. Don't fight it; relax in to the highest state of who you are. Become one with your foreverness.

NOW IS THE TIME TO PERSEVERE

Now it is time to speak of perseverance; the ability to survive. Now is the time to preserver. Now is the time to continue the cycle of love-life on Earth. This is a time of changing energy. You are in control. What do you want? What do you expect? The answers to those questions are what you will get. If you think and believe a certain answer- that is what you will draw to you. Draw peace; it is the desire of the whole of all that is. Of this you are a part of. Draw to you and to your planet the love of which you hold. Stay focused, enjoy, be a part of the love that you are. Any straying from the path will only take you more time, more incarnations, more experiences before reaching your destination. Straying isn't a problem or a solution, just a different path. You won't be judged; there is no right or wrong. All roads will eventually lead to infinite love. Love of the whole that is- which is life. If you want to cut corners, then cut the dramas and go straight to love. You are here for a reason. Make it work in your favor and in the favor of all.

Live for peace. Live for love. Make it a choice. Make it a life. You are valued and we thank you for your participation.

TAKE A TRUTHFUL LOOK AT WHERE YOU ARE GOING

Now is a good time to view the effects of your actions. What did you create so far? What will you continue to create? Are you on your desired path towards a peaceful existence? Now is a good time to take a look and possibly make adjustments- little tweaks here and there, or maybe massive landslides of change are necessary. Take a truthful look. Having great wealth or popularity is not what you should be looking for. Wealth and love- popularity are wonderful to have but they are not your goal. You are here to create the positive energy of love. Did you, have you? Would you like to create more?

We celebrate you because we know that everyone on earth has created sparks of positive energy. Most of you have created both positive and negative energy- both acceptance and judgments. As you weave yourself through this life time you are delivering gifts to yourself, to others, and to your planet. What is your gift? Start with yourself. Have you learned that you are a part of living foreverness? That means you are a part of love. Have you learned to live from that place, even when confronting fear? Have you learned that this incarnation is not all there is for your spirit? Practice knowing these things. As you do, expand your loving self to those around you. Expand your goodness, your love. Expand your laughter, and your joy. Make it contagious. We know that you are capable and we know that you have the intellect. We also know that you have a thought, a belief, a desire and an action. The result is up to you. We suggest that, every once in a while, you question your motive. Were you motivated by love or revenge, love or fear, love or sorrow, love or hate? Check in with yourself occasionally. Where is your energy on any particular situation? Where are you now?

We aren't asking for you to be perfect. We are asking for you to be aware. Awareness includes a result. You are in charge. Your awareness will affect your decisions. Your peace and the peace of Earth is up to you. That is all.

YOU ARE IN CONTROL OF EARTH'S ENERGY
It is now time to say that you are in control. The energy of Earth has changed. No longer is there a need for dark spots and separation. Everyone is needed and everyone, in their own way

can and will contribute to everlasting peace and love. YOU are a participant. What energy are you bringing forward? Will it be the energy for the one-celled amoebas or for the highly evolved intellectuals? Both forms are seeking the same substance- the energy of life-love-foreverness. You, and them are energy. The energy will survive. The physical embodiment of this energy is in question. Earth has evolved. Will human kind allow it to continue? Only peace will be the answer. Peace will defer natural disaster and manmade disaster. The energy of peace will be the savior of Earth.

Have we made our point? Is our position clear to you? We the teachers, who have walked in physical form on Earth, are sharing a view. YOU are in our lens. You are the Now Guardians of earth. It is with love that we give you our trust. You are the chosen ones for now. Your successors will continue in your footsteps. Will they be walking towards or away from infinite love? How did you lead?

SEE YOUR GOODNESS IN THE REFLECTION OF YOUR SURROUNDINGS

We see the beauty and we want you to see it also. Instead of looking at what is going wrong and maybe participating in the wrongness, we encourage you to look at what is going right. Stay focused on the amount of caring, joyfulness, laughter, and love that you see and maybe in which you are participating. Comment on the goodness you see. Bring awareness to others of the goodness you see. Focus more on the wellness, and less on the sickness. Take time out to look at what is going right for you or has gone right or will go right. And when you see it, give thanks. Express gratitude- which is a calling for more goodness.

We give thanks for you. It is with love that we celebrate your contributions to the forward movement of Earth. If we can see the goodness in you, maybe you can see the goodness in you and in others. It is there. Goodness is in everyone because everyone is made of the infinite particles of love, of life. Look for the goodness in each other and look less for the badness in each other. It is all there, in plain sight. By looking for the goodness, you will be expanding positive energy for the survival of Earth. Do you see the great connection between your joyfulness and love, and the survival of Earth- which also feels the love-life? All is connected- you others and Earth. What affects one will affect the others. See the effect you have. See your goodness in the reflection of your surroundings. We want you to know that you are the vision of hope and survival. Now it is your turn.

WILL YOU CONTRIBUTE TO THE LIFE OR DEATH OF EARTH?

We the teachers are offering you these words of truth. These truths are our offerings of hope. Earth and all of its life is our mission. You the people are the saviors or destroyers of Earth. Through the use of your energy, you have the power of attracting to Earth both life and death. Now is a good time for awareness of your thoughts, beliefs, actions and your energy.

We believe that you are ready. We believe the people of Earth want the continuation of their planet. If that is true for you, what will you do about it? How will you increase the positive energy for you and for your planet? It won't do much good to shake your finger at each other in judgment. The best actions that you can take would be to listen from within and follow your inner truth- the real truth. You can always recognize a real truth by its energy. A real truth will always be in a state of positive energy. The "real" truth is connected to infinite energy, and infinite energy is the connection to all that is. "All that is" is connected to every life form, every star, every planet, and every galaxy. Forever is larger than you can imagine, and it has the same connection to infinite energy that you have. You- and us are all a part of the same system of forever energy of life. Tune in at any time. Expand this energy on Earth with your happiness, love, joy, giggles and grins.

We want you to know that you are all participants. More often than not, will you be attracting the love and life of earth or the death of Earth. What will it be?

VISUALIZE PEACE ABOVE ALL ELSE

We believe in the possibility of a peaceful planet Earth. We understand the journey. Can you visualize the path? Are you willing to move in that direction? Moving in the direction of peace will mean that many of you will have to give up your beliefs which do not align with a unified planet. Becoming open to new ways of thinking and being will take adjustment. Are you willing? We suggest that you start with smaller increments. Start with desire and awareness. Alignment will begin once you accomplish desire and begin working through the levels of awareness. Those two increments can take a lifetime to accomplish. Now is a good time to begin. Know that you are here in body on Earth with the purpose of expanding positive energy. The expansion of HEF will include all- every life form. All of earth is alive.

If you desire peace for all of earth, consider your adjustments? Are you willing to give up negative energy frequencies? You may have found satisfaction in promoting dramas, jealousies, hording, blaming, suffering, or harming. Are you ready to give it up? Are you ready to change into positive energy? Do you want to feel self love, joy, and happiness? If so, then let go of the negative energy. Stop being a part of what you don't want. If your relationship ends, stop the drama. Move on to more love. If you are lonely, stop the judgment. Get up and enjoy one another. If you are poor, stop the woe-is-me. Get up and experience the richness of life. Eventually, walls of perceived protection will break down. Free flowing movements of love will enter. Expansion into your desire will begin. Become one with your desire. Become one with peace. We want you to know that peace is the outcome of letting go. Visualize peace above all else.

FOCUS ON YOUR MOVEMENT- YOUR JOY

We the teachers, we the people of Earth, are gathered to express our joy. We are here to say that your joy is our joy. The joy of all transmits to the energy of all. Are you laughing or crying, hugging or pushing away? Are you a good listener or do you interrupt, which means, do you try to understand even if you aren't in the same place? What gets your attention? Are you moved by loving kindness, intelligence, power, the weak or the strong? Our suggestion is to fine tune your path. Can you see the love in everyone? If not, look deeper within your self love. Look for what is usually unnoticed- the desire for loving acceptance. Your desire for acceptance is the same as all. Your path to acceptance is individualized. Stop the judgment. Everyone is on the same path to infinite love. Everyone has a reason for the path they are on. Become one with the paths. Accept the differences. Rejoice in knowing that every spirit came into physical form to grow towards infinite love. That is enough. No more is needed than to grow towards infinite love. They need not be more rich, more powerful, more understanding, more loving. They are here for the experiences of expanding infinite love. Let them be. To do so, spend more time in expanding your own personal loving self.

Now is a good time to view the inner part of you. Look inside, and feel the love within. If you look at *them*, and feel contempt, then the contempt is you without joy. We are asking that, instead, you focus on joy. Change your focus from what *they* are not experiencing to what you are not experiencing. Then change your experience to loving acceptance of yourself. By doing so, you will be able to lovingly accept them. Do you get this? Are you beginning to understand that love and joy are about you first? Once you get it, you will see it in others. Begin to view the differences as being the same- just on a different path. Everyone is moving towards infinite love. Focus on your movement, your joy. Let it be.

VISUALIZE A NEW EARTH

We will talk about the scene from a new earth- sounds a bit like science fiction. The difference is, The New Earth can be true, not fiction. The new Earth is a desired place to live. The New Earth can look like utopia, heaven, and paradise. All that is needed is love, kindness, joy, happiness, gratitude.... Earth already has all the other necessary ingredients. Earth has atmosphere, air, water, seasons, mountains, lakes- beauty beyond description. Have you taken a look around lately? Did you see the magnificent colors, patterns, and beauty? Have you noticed your breath lately and paid attention to the air of life that you breathe? What we are suggesting is that you take moments each day to see the beauty of your planet and to give thanks. Be grateful for the paradise that you live in. Thanks and gratitude are a part of creating the scene from a new Earth.

Next, The New Earth will need much love. Oh there is plenty of loving energy surrounding the planet and living in every life form, yet in order to maintain life, love will have to be acknowledged, cultivated and shared. Love is a simple recipe for a prosperous planet. Humans must feel and share love, to prevent the decay into devastation. You can see it happening in places throughout this otherwise wonderful planet. Anyone can understand the look of a loveless place. Anyone can also understand the look of a loving world. If you drew a picture of a loving planet, what would it look like? Try it right now. Draw the picture in your mind. Draw the scene from a New Earth.

While you are at it, add people and animals to the scene. Did you add happiness and joy to the people and animals? We hope so because that is the key to survival of Earth. Loving people, not fighting people will learn to live together, share together, and come together for the prosperity of Earth. We believe in you, along with your ability and desire to have a flourishing vibrant planet.

All you have to do is live from your truth, your loving self. Your fictional self is not attached to your forever self. For the sake of human kind and of planet Earth, we ask that you recognize the difference between fact and fiction, love and fear, abundance and greed. Now is a good time to visualize a New Earth.

EXPERIENCE THE MOVEMENT OF LOVING PEACE

We will begin by saying that the end is near. The end is- of the way it was- and the beginning of the way it will be. There is an abundance of energy in the direction of a loving, peaceful Earth; too much to let slip away. There is a massive movement erupting in areas across the planet. The movements are positive and truthful. They are not built on human made beliefs of separation. The movements are for the unity of all life on Earth. Isn't that good news? Do you feel encouraged by knowing there is a movement of peace on Earth? The words "Peace On Earth" are becoming a reality, not just a meaningless phrase.

In this Time of Now, Earth will experience a change. The movement is already in motion. You are a participant. Your energy of thoughts, beliefs, and actions are in play. We are excited to see the participants already in action, and to see the curious looking on. For some, there will be denial for a few more

154

life times, yet eventually all will join in. For as long as the prevalent energy of earth is positive, movement will continue towards a peaceful, planet for all. Now we encourage you all to take a look- sneak a peek at the possibilities. For as long as you can, experience a peaceful, loving world. Try it. Join the flow and feel the difference. That means to let go of all your sorrow stories, your dramas, your fears, and for awhile experience loving peace. You can do it- if only for awhile. Eventually, your short term loving peace will develop into long term conditions of life. Then truly, you are on the path.

We invite you to give it a try. For a while, for as long as you can hold on to it, experience loving peace. It is yours as a gift. The gift you receive will be the same gift that you give to the planet. All for one.

THE POWER OF KEEPING YOU AND EARTH ALIVE

It is now time to realize that you have the power for the survival of Earth. Along with this power is your spiritual journey towards the love of all that is. That is to say, as Earth heals so does your spirit and so do all of the spirits who enter the physical realm to help earth to heal. It is a big project and well worth the undertaking. There is much gratitude for the billions of souls who will be participating. Imagine all the light energy coming to earth. You can view it as orbs or... lightening bugs. It is with love that light energy comes to earth; not only as humans but also as animals and plants. Each comes to help the other. Our suggestion is to not feel above or below another life form. Know that each is on the same mission of sustainability of life/love. Are you a team player? No matter the role you are playing, all is for the greater purpose of love/life.

Your role is no greater or lesser than another life form. All will be born and will die for the purpose of love. Every spirit will ascend the physical body, returning to love. Every physical body and brain will drive the organism through the physical process... you, the bug, the mosquito, the bird.... All play a role. Life sustains life. Love sustains life. Nothing more is needed. Your planet is alive, give gratitude and keep the love flowing. We thank you.

THE DISCOVERY OF A MUTUAL RELATIONSHIP- HEART AND BRAIN

Now is another opportunity to talk about discovery. The discovery we have in mind is to discover what is in your heart area? Your heart area is the center of connection to all that is; your connection to love. Discover your life line. Life will be easier for you once you discover your connection and then start living from that connection. You see, your connection is to all that is, and to those who will help you- especially in the spirit world. Your head, your brain, is for moverability (did we make up that word) through the physical world. We know that your brain is important for getting you from birth to death. Can you imagine how much easier it would be if the brain connected to the heart area (infinite love)? What if you were able to let go of what didn't matter in the physical world? A lot of the energy that you use doesn't get you further towards peace. Often the opposite is true. Your energy and emotions sometimes lead you away from peace. Now is a good time to discover the differences in movement towards and away. Once again, it is your choice. Wallow in the undesired or be guided towards the desired. Your heart area, your connection to all, will lead if you allow. Now is the time to let your love/heart/guides lead your physical brain. Let them work together- as they were meant to do. Don't close out one for the other. Stay with your connection to all that is. Stay in your body and stay in your spirit. Be mutual friends discovering each other.

156

YOU AND YOUR ENERGY ARE IMPORTANT

We are very excited to begin speaking about forever love; also known as infinite love, god, source, the whole and any other name you may have. For us, we are talking about a frequency. There is much to be said about this frequency which is the provider of all life in all of forever. Do you find that to be interesting and exciting? We hope so. This energy is all about you, who you are, where you live and the space around you- the space that goes on forever, past your imagination. We find it to be exciting that you are a part of it all. YOU! Probably you were unaware of your importance to the greater picture. Probably you felt insignificant and could easily go into HEF (high energy frequency) or LEF (low energy frequency) for no particularly large importance. We can assure you that all energy you emit is contributing to the whole. Low energy- fear, anger, jealousy, revenge, greed... happens. Try not to spend much time in this wasted place. Move as quickly as possible to high energy. In time and with practice, you will be able to live without low energy frequencies. Believe in the possibility of never dipping below neutral. That means, believe that you can always live in joy, happiness, love, or neutrality. Practice. It will be. We want you to know that you are important and so is your energy.

THE SOONER YOUR GET THIS, THE SOONER YOUR PEACE

It is time for a quick review. You are loved and you give love to others and to your planet. Your love is necessary for the continuation of life. It is that simple. Parts of the high frequency energy of life are energies of peace, joy, happiness- which fade into contentment, pleasures, and a sense of well-being.

That is the review. Now, the question often spoke is, "how do I get there"? The answer as always is to choose high energy over low energy, no matter what your circumstances. That means to elevate yourself into love instead of fear. Practice. After a while of knowing your self-love, the process will become automatic. When this begins to happen, give thanks. Rejoice. Keep up the happy work. For those of you in heavy suffering, take a break as often as you can. Break into laughter for no particular reason; break into silliness, or into knowing of your greatness. Take a break by reminding yourself that you can- at any time you choose. You are not destined to suffer throughout the eternity of this incarnation. Neither is your spirit destined to suffer throughout eternity. Your spirit is destined toward love. Every spirit, without exception is destined towards love. No matter what you have experienced in this incarnation, you are still on the path to love- to high frequency- to all that is, which is who you are. Give your brain a break from the suffering. Know that you are a part of forever. Love is forever and love is life. The sooner you get this, the sooner you will be on your way- in this incarnation, to peace.

THE HIGHER FREQUENCIES OF FOREVER ENERGY

We know who you are; you are the keepers of forever energy. We say the keepers because you in physical form have the ability to manipulate the energy. What you use is what you grow. Use a lot of negative energy- increase the negative energy on Earth. We think that maybe your didn't mean to use so much negative energy. That maybe you weren't thinking or paying attention to your "down-ness" Take a closer look. See and recognize your interpretation of your experiences. Pay attention to your responses. Respond with love. If someone is beating you, feel the love within you. That is your connection to a greater source. Be aware of the anguish the beater is experiencing. Simply, be aware of your love and his hurt- your love, his fear. Know that the experience is temporary. You are eternal. Your pain is short term, your love is forever. Yes, while hell is breaking out for you, know your place. Continue to connect with your inner love. The truth is, by doing so your pain and suffering will be less. We recognize how difficult this may sound. Remember- we too have walked in flesh on Earth and have felt pain and suffering. The fastest way to relief is through love. You are love no matter what your situation.

And now, knowing that you are love, proceed in the direction of high energy frequency. More often than not, and with conscious awareness, stay in the neutral area or above- whatever the event. At first, do this by conscious choice. Eventually, staying above negative energy will become automatic.

You have the power to manipulate your energy- your feelings. Choose the best- choose the higher frequencies of forever-energy. You, your neighbors, your country and your world will be in a better place when living the best energies for survival.

YOU ARE THE LEADER, WHAT IS YOUR PLATFORM?

Now. We are here to show you the view of a greater tomorrow; the view that you all can see and direct. Each of you is the directors of this scene. There is no one higher or above you to produce tomorrow's world. Your country's leaders are not responsible. The responsible leaders are the ones with the visions and the desire for a peaceful, loving planet. There are many of you. Once again, we suggest that you join together whenever possible. It will be the people who make the changes, not the current world leaders. Don't blame and accuse them for the role they are in.

Someone has the job of peace keeper- many someones. Those who are connected to the love within, who more often than not live in the higher frequencies are the change makers. We are now looking at the leaders of the change makers. Are you a leader in change? We are here to help you. Talk to us as often as you choose. Talk and listen through prayer and meditation. Prayer is the voicing of your intent, meditation is getting still inside and ready to receive. Both can happen anywhere, and any time. Prayer and meditation works perfectly well wherever you are at any time. We always hear you, and we guide you- even when you are unaware. Bring to yourself awareness of being heard and guided. Accept that we are with you.

And now, the world you will be creating- can you see it, imagine it, and move closer toward it. This new world is probably a part of your present world. Amidst all the chaos is peace. Develop the habit of looking for it. The more you see and experience the peace and love around you, the more you will be able to lead others in that direction. The more you are able to see and experience, the more you will "be" in that place. Your "being" is the teacher- the leader. When you are "being" in a loving, high frequency energy, you won't be hurting others, or judging, or blaming.

What we want you to know is that you are a leader for the new way of Earth. What will be your platform? We are excited to hear about it.

DISCOVER THE TRUTH BY ADJUSTING YOUR FOCUS

Within the realm of truth, a new discovery is upon you. The new discovery is a place of limitless space and ideas. The limitless space is something that you can discover within. In time, everyone will open to the idea of their connection to all. Just as scientists have discovered physical matter that connects Earth to all, there will be a discovery that connects life and spirit to all. That discovery is not so far away. For now, hold on to the possibility and begin living *as if*. Live as if you are connected to all, just as the physical planet of earth is a part of all. The only difference is size. Physical Earth matter is large and seeable, spiritual energy matter is small and invisible to most of the physical eyes. Both exist anyway. The discovery will happen.

We want you to know that science is catching up to the truths-even though science will slip and slide along the way. The truth is in plain sight- it isn't in hiding. The truth is that all will be revealed when people are opened to the unveiling. Now is a good time to adjust your focus. Clue- Aim towards infinite love.

HEALING IS IN YOUR CONTROL

And now, we will say that the healing of yourself, your community, your country, your planet is in the hands of those who *know*. Healing is in YOUR hand. There is a not a supreme being-spirit in the afterlife to save you. We, your guardians can guide but we can't save you. Your government leaders and military are not saviors either. The "saving" is about transforming your negative energy into loving energy. Yet, because your core of existence is love- high frequency, you already contain all the "saving" you need. While on earth, you are free to experience all of the earthy conditions, both desirable and undesirable. Throughout your incarnations, you will be having all the experiences. Once your spirit leaves its temporary body, the spirit will not be judged for its adventures.

The difference between NOW and past centuries is that the process can be speeded up. Instead of spending so much time in negative energy, pain, and suffering know that people have developed. The knowledge and ability is available for living in high frequencies of peace. Imagine all the sickness that will disappear- so will the hunger and the need for shelter when people begin to live together as one unit, one planet.

What we want you to know are that now, the road to peace is more available than ever before. It is your choice to struggle or to go in the direction of peace. This requires an internal change brought on by desire. Healing will be brought on by your desire.

YOUR GOD

It is time that you hear about a loving god- which is something that has been contemplated throughout centuries. The clue is what you call god. Are you speaking of an iconic man who lives in the sky and the afterlife? Are you talking about an energy source, an all that is, the whole, infinite love.... How did you come to define your loving god? Did it, he, she, expand infinitely into the whole? Did it, she, he, include everyone and everything in its loving wholeness? Did you have a choice of the loving god? If so, what did you choose? If you didn't have a choice, who did?

What we want you to know is that everyone's loving god is a part of everyone's loving core. Doesn't that make it simple? Isn't it better to be all inclusive than to be divided in war, anger, beliefs? We tell you that it is true. Your god, and your god, and your god, is the god within, which is the god of love, which is another name for the highest energy frequency of love, life, foreverness.

Of course your god is a god of love. By any name or any resemblance, you are one and the same of the god of love. Now is a good time to come together and start acting from your god of love. Now is a good time to come together in joy, happiness, love, and acceptance. And that is all that is. Let it be.

"LET IT BE" HAS MEANING

The Books Of Now are for the purpose of enlightenment. We aren't here to argue or persuade. It isn't our job to convince. It is our job to deliver the message, the truths. It is up to you, the human, to accept, challenge, or reject. Let it be.

And now, we present to you the idea of your place in forever. Being born and living a physical existence has very little to do with your foreverness. In fact, being in physical form is a piece of your foreverness- but not the whole. The total of YOU is much more than years on Earth. You are much greater than a few years. Your experiences are vast in a never ending- shall we say galaxy. Not the right word but- how to say a place larger than you can imagine. You all are creators of this foreverland. You are bits and pieces of all that is. Each seed becomes a great plant. So do you. It is time now to estimate your power as a seed of forever. You are the generator of much to come. We recognize the sounding and importance of that statement. We recognize the glory and the power within- you. The glory and the power forever- are you. Pick up the courage to be you because YOU are the power and the glory of forever. Let it be. We ask of you to let it be. LET IT BE has a real meaning, the meaning is to allow.

With all that is and all that comes, we ask that you see your place in foreverland. You are the seed. You are the plant. You are a piece of forever. Allow your greatness; allow your love to flow. Let you be.

ENJOY THE NEW VIEW

We are here to say that the best is yet to come. Come with us to view the adventure, the love, the joy, of forever. You will have to do this in your mind's vision or in your time travel. Both are possible, and very similar. Now, view your Earth and your people as you currently see it. Look at the happy, the sad, the wanted and the unwanted. Spend some time looking around inside your mind. Look at the whole planet as best you can. If you had a magic wand, would you change anything? We are going to suggest that you are the magic and your body is the wand. Now, what will you change? The answer is that you will change what you desire to be different. That is your power. Of course your question will be "how can I change the- world, country, city, neighborhood, family"? The answer is in your belief. Do you believe in energy? Do you believe that you are in physical form? Can you believe that you can manipulate energy- you can move it? If yes, then that is your answer. You have the ability to create the world of your dreams. As a guide, we say that you can be assured; other humans want the same dream to be created. Our suggestion is to start along the path. Soon you will meet up with others on the same path. Enjoy the meet-up, and encourage conversation. This is how YOU will be aligning with change. Start with a desire, begin walking towards it, and join with others on the same path.

Once you walk the path in your mind and changes begin to happen, your view will change. Instead of seeing poverty, you will see richness. Instead of seeing lack you will see the abundance. Actually, you will not only be seeing the change but you will be experiencing the difference. Take notice.

Enjoy the difference of the new world. Now is the time to experience the difference. Make it a choice.

LIGHT UP YOUR WORLD WITH POSITVE ENERGY

Are you ready for the adventure? The script is written and now it is your time to experience the event. You see, you are here on Earth to experience the fullness of your being. You can experience it in way you choose. That is to say that you can choose how you will be experiencing your life. You can't choose all the events but you can choose all of your interpretations and responses. The energy of you and Earth will be affected by your response. We are looking for a positive response with an increase in positive energy. Your choice though. The events you witness will have no meaning until you apply one. The events will have no emotion- you will be the provider. Now is your turn because now is when you are here on Earth in physical form. Now is when you are the dream maker. What are you creating? No matter the content of the dream, will you make it about love, joy, happiness or will you make it a nightmare? The dream is your earthly reality.

Your reality is based on your interpretation. We suggest you take a closer look at how you view yourself and Earth. Keep those rosy colored glasses and wear them regularly. Really though, you can view the same issue as either rosy, or grey. Your choice.

It is time now to lift a dark veil. It is time for the energy of Earth to become brighter. You are the light- the bright maker. Begin seeing the positive side of change. We want you to know this is your mission- to light up the world with positive energy.

TILTING THE ENERGY TOWARDS PEACE

It is in our scope of knowledge to say that the time has come for peace. By having peace, one also has self love, self joy, self happiness, etc. Are you ready? Are you willing to give up your war games, your greed, your suffering? For some the answer is yes, for others the answer is no. We understand. Readiness will happen in intervals. Everyone is moving forward at their own pace. It is time for everyone to understand that the glory, the joy, the love will happen when Earth's energy reaches the next tilt. We think this is exciting and we hope you do too. All that is needed is a bit more excitement, a bit more joy, love, compassion and realization that YOU are the tilt maker.

Go inside now to your heart space. Is now a good time? Open up to the idea that you are tilting the energy of Earth towards peace. Yes, you all will eventually add to the tilt. For now, some will, others will contemplate or resist. Some have broken down barriers; others still cling to walls of perceived safety. We understand. Those walls were built because of past experiences; Many years in past experiences of survival. It's over. Release to the newness of peace. Trust in the adventure. Now is the time for your peace and for peace on Earth. We will be with you throughout the transition. Depend on us in times of need- in times for comfort as you let go. You are never alone. Not Ever.

INCREASE THE FLOW OF A PROSPEROUS PLANET

Let's get to the point of your presence on Earth. The point is that you are a part of a vast system which continues the flow of life. Just as the moon continues the flow of Earth's seasons, so do the people continue the flow of life. Now is the time to pick up the pace a bit. That is to say that now it is time for positive energy to increase. You are the ones who will open the valves allowing more positive energy throughout the planet. You are also the ones who will close down the valves on the flow of negative energy.

Let's move forward. We believe that you understand the concept of energy, and the difference between positive and negative energy. We believe you understand your purpose of being in physical form on Earth. The concept of love has been talked about for thousands of years. The same is true for the concept of peace and joy. Now is a perfect time to increase the momentum and bring forth the reality.

This is the time to recognize and feel the abundance of an overflowing planet. There is plenty of all that you need here on Earth. Wake up to the bounty and give thanks. Whether your table is full or empty, there is still enough. When everyone begins to wake up to love and peace, every table will be full. Your planet is a generous provider. The hoarding can stop and the sharing can increase. To make this a reality, know it, feel it, believe it, and act accordingly. If you are the poor person on the side of the road, wake up and *know* there is enough for you. Believe in enough. If you are the wealthy person, wake up to the idea of changing the rules for sharing. Begin with sharing from your heart space which is always self refilling. Your loving kindness will never run dry unless you turn off the valve.

Now is the time to view the flow of a prosperous Earth. Open the valve from your heart space. There is always enough.

VISUALIZE THAT WHICH YOU EMIT TO THE WORLD

Now we want to talk about the end result- the conclusion of your efforts. What we want to see is a chain reaction into future generations. You see, it is now that the ball has started rolling. It is now that the momentum is gaining. When we say momentum, what we mean is that we can see the energy and the color and know the direction. Some of you in physical form can also *see* the energy. Some people or scientist use specialized equipment to see. We are pleased- pleased that you care enough to look for the direction of earth's energy. We certainly hope you will always have awareness. It is also true that we can tell the wellness of the people, plants, and animals of earth by looking at the wellness colors of earth.

Know that your energy is magnified as it goes out and away from your body. What we mean is that your energy is not consumed within a physical body. It reaches much further past your physical existence. If others in physical form could see your energy (which some people can do), what would you want them to see? If your body expels gas while you walk about, what color would you want it to be? What we are saying is, become aware of what you emit.

Visualize your opportunity to expel, radiate, emit, and shine that which the next generation and the future of earth needs to experience. Now, while it is your turn, shine throughout forever.

BE YOU AND GIVE THANKS

We find it to be exciting that YOU are here for the cause of creating peace. Oh we are sure that many of you know your cause and some of you never will while in this incarnation. Yet, you are still present and so is your cause. We are still delighted to be here with you all. It is certainly more uplifting than the past few thousand years on Earth. A wonderful change is upon Earth and you all are experiencing and contributing to the change. It is your contributions that will propel the planet forward into the next generations and hundreds of years- which is a short time in the eternity of foreverland.

Your mission is to create the love which will maintain the survival of your planet. Once again, when we say the word love we recognize that it is an overused term with an insufficient connotation. We suggest that you use the term love to expand onto the highest, cleanest, most clear energy. See past your horizon. See a universal, a galactic and infinite love which is the same as life. See the ultimate energy of all that is. You don't have to see it; you can experience the energy of life- of love. Experience the essence of YOU. Rejoice when you find the essence of love within. Rejoice when you find the essence of love which has nothing to do with another physical object. Rejoice with knowing that you are the love and you are the connection to all that is. Know that you are the savior and the energy of always. Be you and give thanks.

WE, THE TEACHERS, UNDERSTAND

There is still much to say and much hope for planet Earth. It is with great love that we deliver the messages for the Now Books. We the Teachers are optimistic that people on Earth will study the writings and practice the messages. We see the glow of Earth; we see the light in each person. We know that there is a path and that eventually everyone will complete the journey. We are grateful for you all.

We understand that at any particular time, a person may be in high frequency or in low frequency- it is all a part of the path. What we hope you will recognize is that you don't have to stay or be stuck in frequencies that you don't like. You have choices. The more you choose high frequencies, the more you will receive high frequencies. When unwanted events happen, recognize it for what it is and move on. Take your time to grieve or be angry, but don't get stuck... move on to joy. You have the power to move on to better energy. Use it. Exercise your power. Become aware of your energy- which can mean your frequency or your thoughts and feelings. Become a manipulator. Manipulate yourself, and your planet with an energy of choice. You can do it. You have the power. Become aware of your energy, and guide it.

BRING AWARENESS TO YOUR POWER

One of the best things you can do for yourself, your family, country, and planet is to become aware of your power. It is within you to have all that is available in your world- and that is a lot. Your world offers more than anyone needs. It is now time to share the wealth, the realignment, and the glory for all. As a united planet, the high frequency energy will increase. Earth will become a safe planet for billions more years. Let it be.

Let the love reign on Earth. That means to let the life of Earth remain. It is in your hands. Don't doubt your power and don't discard your power. Act on it. Act for the purpose of life. Now is your time to be a healer. All of life can heal with the power of positive energy. That is a fact.

We are here as your assistants in the healing program. Rely on us. Let us help. Together, the energy from those in physical bodies and from those in spiritual forms can act as a team on behalf of Earth. What we are saying is for each of you to bring awareness to the energy of you, others, and the world. It is still your turn.

EXPERIENCE YOUR GREATNESS THROUGH YOUR LOVING SELF

And now, it is our pleasure to reassure you of your greatness. This is the time to live from the very best part of you. Go ahead, enjoy, you have nothing to lose in the big picture and so much fun to experience when you choose to live in joyful, loving, moments. It will help for you to believe in you and your good words about yourself. Live from your loving self and disregard all else. Try it for awhile- a bit each day. Practice until your joyfulness becomes a habit. Live your dream in the right now. The dream, the goal, the plan is to live joyfully. It is up to you to make the dream come true. No one else will be responsible for your joy. No one can. Your love, your happiness comes from your connection. You feel the connection from your heart space. No matter what is going on in your world, spend more time living from your heart space. Try to laugh in the face of danger. Try to view your world from your strongest connection. Looking at the same issue, the view is a lot different in high energy than it is in low energy. Take time to refocus when necessary. After all, it is your own personal view. You have the power to view your life in your world in any way you choose. No one can be in the way of your loving connection to all that is.

For a moment, right now, take some time, at least a few minutes to experience your loving connection. While doing so, take a look around inside your mind. Whatever you are seeing, shine on it the light of love. Whatever you view in your mind, can be viewed with love. What you experience in the physical world can be

170

experienced with the consciousness of love. Don't pass up the opportunities to be all that you can. Be your loving self.

MORE ABOUT YOUR POWER OF LOVE-LIFE

It is now time to say more about the messages of Love-Life, HEF. The messages of survival are for the humans, and planets and animals of Earth. You, the humans have the power to decimate life on Earth. That is a powerful place to be. We hope you will take this seriously. The person(s) who pulls the triggers or pushes the button to destroy are only partially responsible. Everyone else has contributed one way or another to the positive or the negative energy of Earth. Become aware of your energy. Check in with yourself regularly. Where is your energy? Make a habit of noticing and adjusting when necessary. Keep in mind that adjusting your energy has very little to do with the events going on around you. It really has to do with keeping your energy high through all events. Work at it. Practice.

Now, while you practice awareness of your energy, at the same time, you will be adjusting the energy of Earth. As all the energy becomes more positive, the chances of devastation decrease. Do you see how you are a contributor? Do you see that you and others producing the same energy can ignite a fuse? The ignition will be the positive or the negative that you chose to use. Take this seriously.

Become the energy of life- become HEF. In your heart space, breathe in the greatest power of all. Breathe in to infinite love. Then begin noticing the changes surrounding you. Notice that you are creating the change for a more positive Earth. Notice that the energy of love is more powerful than the hand that pulls the trigger or pushes the button to devastate. And while you are noticing your HEF and infinite love within, give thanks for your greatest power and connection to all that is- the energy of life, the whole. Let It Be.

GO WITH THE NATURAL FLOW- THE BREATH OF LIFE

And now we are ready to talk about the comings and goings; the expansions and the collapsing of the energy of earth. You can view it as the inhale and the exhale of your breath; the filling of your lungs and the expulsions from your lungs. Such is the energy around you and your planet. At any time, you can breathe in and breathe out of this energy. Actually, you do it all the time. It is your support- your life and the life of Earth. If only you could see on a much smaller scale, you would see the breathing, the using, the inhale and exhale of energy. All of life does this- including the wholeness of your planet.

What we encourage is for you to allow the continuation of the process. Your may not be aware of the times of suffocation. We can tell you that the light dims or goes out when the energy is negative. We see it regularly with those who suffer and in those who create suffering. Whether you consider yourself the wounded or the person wounding, the energy is the same. Become aware of your energy. Many of you don't realize the result of your positive or negative energy. Become aware. If you are feeling positive, others feel it too. Your energy is free flowing and not suffocating. Your positive energy is life sustaining. Keep it up. The more you give to the energy of life, the more you will receive in return. The giving and receiving is love, joy, happiness. The more you repress these feelings, the more you are shutting off from life, the more you are suffocating- yourself and others.

We suggest you give it up. Go with the natural flow- the breath of life. All you have to lose is the energy you don't need. All you have to gain is the best that is. Give it a try. Rejoice. Rejoice just because you can. As always, it is your choice.

HAVING THE DESIRES OF THE HEART

Now is a wonderful opportunity to visit the desires of the heart. The most popular desire is to feel the presence of love. To feel, to experience, and to embrace love is the single most desired experience of all life forms. The good news is- *that which is desired is always available.* We know that most people will question and disbelieve, yet we say the feeling you most desire is within you. The energy of LOVE doesn't know the difference of coming from another person, a pet, a plant, a child.... The energy of love is blind and deaf. It doesn't need the five senses in which humans are accustomed to using. What will it take for you to understand? How much more clearly can we say that the experience most desired is an energy force which is readily available at all times. All you need to experience this energy that you call love, is to go into your heart space and connect with your infinite source. This may take a lot of practice. Now is a good time to begin.

We don't have a name for this energy that you call love. We know it by the feel. We have learned through practice to live in the light of "love." It is our experience and it can be yours also. As we said, this energy is abundant and surrounds all of life. It is a part of all life; therefore it is a part of you and around you. All you have to do is practice connecting. This energy is even stronger than the love you have for another, and this infinite love won't abandon or cause pain. We strongly recommend spending time learning to connect and experience the greatest love of all. Fulfilling the desires of the heart is an easy path once you believe and practice. What we want you to know is that there is no need to desire what you already have. We understand physical love and infinite love. We recommend going for the best.

Connect with infinite love, self love, and then go for the physical love. You can have it all.

HEART AND BRAIN TEAM UP

Now is a good time to tell you that the best is yet to come. For those of you who are interested, life will be the heaven that you have imagined. Well, at least the heaven of peace, love, prosperity... while still in physical form on Earth. We think that is exciting news. In order to create heaven on earth, go into your heart space, allow your heart space and brain space to interact. Let one talk to the other. The brain uses a learned vocabulary, the heart uses impulses. Not a problem though because the heart has learned to translate the impulses into language- just like Morse code, and binary codes. The two can communicate if you will allow space. Get quiet and allow. Ask questions and listen from your heart space while spirit listens to your brain space. Are you beginning to get it? We are talking about two trains on parallel tracks, both going to the same station called heaven. One train can manipulate the body; the other can manipulate the spirit. One can see the path and navigate; the other can drive the engine. Let's talk about it, team up, and join together for a common path. Your life will be a lot easier and more "heavenly" if you share the load. Become one with body and spirit. You can do so by listening from your word language, your codes, or your energy impulses. Your easiest path will be to keep us in the loop.

THE UNIVERSAL LANGUAGE OF LOVE

We will explain more about intuition and learned body language. We can say that many of you have learned- maybe unconsciously to communicate or read communications without words. When the baby smiles at the parent, no words are needed to understand the communication. Humans have been "trained" to understand without words. Now is a good time to become aware

174

of your training and fine tune it. Now is a good time to be aware and to challenge positive and negative non-verbal communication. Now is a time of awareness. This evolutionary time can be called the Awareness Evolution- even though we don't use words, we feel the awakening. We are experiencing the beginning of an awakening planet. The awakening is to peace. We, along with all the other planets who have awakened, welcome you.

Now it is your turn for your part. Talk about, dream about, live about, and be about peace. If you want peace for your planet, acknowledge your desire and let go of all else. Be the baby and the parent. Know your power and your position. Understand your abilities and your needs. Be aware of your purpose. That is to say, become aware of non-verbal communication. Listen inside.

We are saying that there is a universal language that doesn't use words. This language uses smiles, kindness, laughter, love.... We invite you to join in. From your heart space, experience your love and the love for others. Let it expand.

YOUR LINEAGE

We the teachers are excited to say that you are the choice of tomorrow. What you create today will carry over for thousands of tomorrows. That is a truth. Your energy will not dissipate but in time, new energies will create change. That is to say that if you experience anger today, the anger- negative energy will continue to be available for a very long time. Now let's say that you create joy today. That energy will do the same. But if you create joy today, and for many tomorrows, its presence will become most dominant. Similar to race and genetics, you will always be a part of your ancestors but you will be more of the most prevalent blood line; one part this, ten parts that. In spiritual form blood line is of little concern. In physical form positive and negative energy while on Earth, is more important than anything else. Your energy is important and valued. Your energy will continue life or end life. Do you see the value?

The best lineage you can create is one of peace, joy, love, and happiness.... Pass it along to your children, your grandchildren and your great, great relatives. Pass along the energy of love. And if your picture is hung on the wall in years to come, let it be known as the lineage of greatness, and of love.

Here's to looking at you and your future!

YOUR PURPOSE IN THE REVOLUTION

Are you ready for the discovery track? It is time to discover a perfect you. Once you discover the perfect you, it will be time to live from your perfectness.

You see, the truth is that we are a part of your discovery. We are an instrument in your new learning. We, the messengers, are lighting your inspiration. I think you call it, planting the seed. Either way, we are sending energy thoughts of change. Some of you are ready to receive, others will complete a mission then come back to receive. There is no judgment from us. All will evolve in due time. For now, be reminded that you are the leaders of this new evolution. Some of you are the revolutionaries, some are the victims, and some are the by-watchers. Everyone on earth today is playing a part. Some of you came to die for awareness. Your birth and exit was planned before you began. Others came to blow trumpets in your own way, to bring awareness- trumpets that were noise makers. Those people who clashed with the norm and brought attention to the undesirable. In the end, there will be an understanding of peace.

Many changes will happen. Many laws and rules will be overridden. All of this is necessary for the new view of a peaceful planet. It just so happens that you are here now, in the disheveled time of transition. You are here now to enlighten the cause. In your own way, you will shine the light. We praise you and we thank you for your work.

It is the time now to view your purpose with gratitude. If you are bringing recognition to health, prosperity, abundance, love, torture, violence... let it be known that this is a time of awakening and you are much loved for your contribution. You are needed and appreciated although the physical *you* may not understand. Your planet is growing in to peace for all. It is time and the view is now. Let it be.

TRUTHS AND BELIEFS

Now is a good time to discover the differences in truth; yours, mine, and theirs. You see, we all develop what we consider to be *true* based on our beliefs- those powerful beliefs which we sometimes protect above all else. Are they based in truth? Who said so? Are you willing to evaluate your beliefs- your truths as you know them to be? To challenge your beliefs means you might have to do a bit of soul searching. Hold the belief in the light of your heart space- your connection to all that is, and see what happens. Be still, let go of all thoughts and preconceived ideas. Become a blank mind regarding the belief. This is a good practice for everyone.

Now, as you let go of your belief and your connection to it, allow your inner truth to come through. Don't argue with it, just allow. Make adjustments wherever needed. Hold on to what is right and let go of all else. Allow new beliefs to form. You can do this with most all topics. If necessary, let go of your programming and allow a new script. Challenge yourself to discover a deeper truth. Look at current events in your world. Instead of an automatic belief of one side or the other, let go of taking a side. You just might come up with a whole new story if you listen from within. The new story, the new truth will probably be for the better good of all.

YOU ARE MAKING A DIFFERENCE – THANK YOU

We can see the difference already. We see that the best is coming and you the people of Earth are bringing the change in energy. Some of the view is due to persons bringing attention to the separations in spiritual energy. Some of the view is the reaction to the separations. Keep in mind that some spirits came into the physical plane to give awareness of separation. Whatever the type of violence or suffering that they came to shed a light on, it is working and people are seeing. The reason people are now seeing is that mostly, the evolution has moved far enough to recognize right and wrong, positive and negative energy, and non-judgments. In the Now Times, people are seeing more clearly and reacting from this clearness- or shall we say awareness. Either way, the mind has learned to differentiate and choose between life over death, love over suffering, oneness over separation. Awareness is happening. Because of awareness choices are changing. Choices are leaning towards oneness and a connection to infinite love. We are pleased.

And now, let us remind you that this is your time to look through the lens of awareness. Look towards the larger picture. Look past your personal, individual squabbles. It is a perfect time to look at the energy you are giving to yourself, to others, and to your planet. It is a perfect time to have awareness of energy. It is a perfect time to discover your energy of forever, which means your life and the life of all that is has been around for a long time. The energy will stay around. It is up to you as to how you and your planet will use the energy of life- the energy of forever. We are beginning to see a difference. Are you seeing it too?

EXPERIENCE AND TELL YOUR STORIES OF GREATNESS

Today is a wonderful day to share stories of love, joy, peace, and happiness. We have lots of stories which we see every day. We see many people in physical form enjoying the splendid-ness of their planet. The enjoyment will get easier as time goes on. As more people begin to live in positive energy, the love, joy, peace, and happiness will grow exponentially. Can you imagine? Try to imagine that you are living, more often than not, in a place of good energy. Your imagination is feeding the future so imagine the very best- which is always available. As you imagine, feel it and visualize the best. Experience the best while you are imagining. By doing so you will be helping the best to come.

Now, what about your story? We hope you will regularly take some time to tell your story of love, joy, peace, and happiness. Other people will have similar stories; we hope you will enjoy listening. This is one way for the words of the best to spread. The best life will be the one where everyone lives in positive energy. Now is a good time to create your story by having the experience then talking about it. Experience love and high energy frequencies, then tell others. Exchange smiles during the telling. Are you ready? This is truly a *once-upon-a-time* tale coming true. Experience the best of you and share the greatness.

YOUR TEACHERS, YOUR GUIDES, YOUR PATHS

We the Teachers and your guides believe in you. To make it clear, the Teachers are not the same as your guides. Even though the Teachers offer guidance, they are not as closely connected to each individual as are your guides. You are always loved no matter your circumstances. All of the physical dramas and activity cannot keep you from love. We want you to know this in hopes of you understanding that you are never alone and never without love. It is very important to know that you *are* love because you are a piece of infinite love- infinite life. It can be no other way. You cannot exist without infinite love and infinite life. Your spirit is connected to all that is and all that forever will be. Your body will continue its cycle of all the mass that is. You body is and always will be recycled parts of forever. Nothing new here- just parts of forever. In your darkest moments we cannot save you but we can be with you in love. It may be your path to experience those moments, yet know that you will live on. In your brightest moments we are still with you and celebrating. As a parent loves its child, so do we love you. We can guide, but ultimately the experiences are for you. They are your learning blocks. You will learn about lightness and love. You will learn about darkness and fear. Eventually, you will choose a desired path. Of course it is clear which path will be final, but the number of lessons and life times is up to you. The shortest path is through love... but once again you have the choice of experiencing all the paths. Your life, your lessons, and your paths; we are with you all the way.

NOW IS ALWAYS YOUR TIME

In the moment, NOW is the best time to recognize your greatness. You are here on Earth for a reason. That reason is to magnify your greatness for all of Earth and beyond. You are here now to create the flow of high energy frequencies. This is your time, you are the star. The greatness is within.

Are you aware? Have you recognized your greatness? Have you breathed into the love of forever? You have the ability- and you have the right. You can experience and live from your greatness anytime you desire- anytime you believe. You may have to practice and get used to feeling the love within- the high frequency within. You may have to re-train yourself. You may have to let go of the negative energy with the drama and allow yourself to experience the positive energy. In the end, you can choose between love, joy, happiness, and peace or fear, sadness, war, and misery. You feel it, you experience it, and you choose-free will.

Now, are you ready? Have you accepted your role? Do you still question your power and your position? You have the right to question for always. When you are ready the answers will appear; today, next life time or somewhere in between. Just know, to make the difference, you must be in physical form where you have the mass to move the mountain of energy. Now is always a good time and now will always be present. –With love all the way, The Teachers.

THE ENERGY OF LOVE BY ANY OTHER NAME

Because we know of your greatness and your power, we see greatness coming from you. It is clear that many of you don't see your greatness. It is clear that many of you have been conditioned to see despair. Know that your conditioning of despair was for the benefit of someone who felt less than the whole of all that is. The whole that is love, god, or source, in our words is the highest energy frequency

The clearest, cleanest, non-polluted power that you call love is infinite love. It is a part of you. It is your core. It is your life. It is your existence and the existence of all that is. The glue that binds you to forever and the glue that binds forever are the same. Call it love, god, source, or any name you choose. The energy is of the highest frequency. The time is NOW to know the energy without a name. Experience the greatness. Let go of all else. This is our asking.

THE ERA OF PEACE

We are ready to talk about the beginning and the end of the era of peace. This is the final frontier for Earth. The era of peace is the final destination and this era has begun. At first you will see the clutter and disarray. Like cleaning out your home, the cleaning looks messy, but the final result is pleasing. Such is the beginning and the end. From disarray will come joy. You see, first the darkness needed to be exposed to light. The separation of powerful and powerless needed to be seen in oneself, in the societies, and in the countries. It will take some time to air out the differences before coming together as one planet of peace. The movement has started. Be grateful to all who participate in their own way. The participation will be with people holding negative energy and violence along with people holding the positive light energy of love. View this all as the scenes of change. Watch from your inner place of knowing. There is no need for fear; there is a need to allow.

This is the time to view a changing planet. Within a few hundred years, new books will be written about experiencing the joy, peace and love. Children will grow up in a loving environment and abuse will end. We hope that you will look forward to the changing Earth with joyful anticipation of the outcome. Now is a good time to start the celebrations of a peaceful earth. To celebrate means to dance, sing, smile, laugh- all the fun stuff that spreads positive energy. No need to wait. The beginning is here, join in.

TOGETHERNESS IN INFINITE LOVE

We are ready now to discuss the meaning of togetherness. One person thinks up an idea and shares it with another. One person has a belief and lives by it. One person has commitment and stays with it. Eventually, others will recognize the idea, belief, and commitment and will accept or reject it. Either way, the one person stays on track. The thought, idea, belief, and commitment that originated in your inner connection to all that is, will probably be the longer lasting. Those ideas, beliefs, and commitments which came from your negative emotions will be the shorter lasting. Your loving connection to self will last forever. The other stuff will fade away. In the end, others will connect with the loving part of you. In the end, your togetherness will be based on one inner connection that is connected with another. The connections will be through infinite self and infinite love.

In the end, everyone will be drawn towards the loving connection of all that is. When you find it, you will recognize it as a part of who you have always been. There will be no struggle or desire to leave that part of you. Before you find it, there will be struggles. The easiest path is to come together as one of all that is. Make it an easy trip. Give up the struggle and join with the energy of all that is. Everyone is there, whether or not they know it. You are there too, so make it easier for you and others. Accept your togetherness in infinite love.

PEACE AND LAWLESSNESS

It is within this infinite journey, through love and life, that we celebrate you. You have become the keepers of Earth. Through the willingness to experience and let go of negative energy, the choice was made to accept and live in positive energy. By doing so, Earth will survive. Everyone will know both energy frequencies and everyone will make their decision. In this lifetime or another, every spirit will seek love-peace-life. This is your journey. This was your journey. Accept with much gratitude, the end of abundant negative energy. Accept peace and positive energy on Earth. You who came forth in physical form are the energy changers. We applaud you. The best is yet to come because you created the possibility.

It was so simple. Without all the rules and regulations, without all the laws and limits, was love. Whew. Doesn't that make it easier? Without all the judgments, and the law enforcement, there was love. A law-less community *can* exist without danger. The time is coming when people will desire to live in peace, not in struggle. Join in. A little at a time, within your comfort zone, dip your toes into peaceful waters. Stretch the idea of goodness in everyone. Begin living without fear. Begin living in love and peace. It can happen and the choice is yours. *Peace will happen, with or without your readiness; in this life time or the next.* Now is a good time to start practicing the acknowledgement of a peaceful Earth. You hold the power. What are you choosing?

YOU ARE ALWAYS CONNECTED TO INFINITE LOVE

We are ready now to tell you about forever love; the love of forever, also known as infinite love. Let it be known that you exist in this realm. You cannot be excluded from the love of forever. No matter what your current experience, or any experience while in physical body, your spirit- your infinite self is always and always will be attached and a part of the high energy frequency of love. We don't call it love. We feel the frequency. So does your spirit. It has been said that you or someone has a "broken spirit." The pain and suffering is deep. We say that the spirit may be experiencing the depth of despair and it feels broken. Yet, your connection to high frequency love is NEVER BROKEN. Understand. No one or no amount of experiences while in physical body can break that connection. Impossible. Your desire to experience more negative energy can come to an end; therefore you may terminate your physical adventure. That is understandable. With birth and death your spirit is always connected and you are always a piece of all that is. Know that you are forever and always will be. Know that, in the end you will be one with the energy of always. Now is your turn to shift energy as best you can. Eliminate the suffering by shifting to joyfulness. No matter what your situation, shift to higher frequency. It is up to you- and you- and you. Because you are in physical form with the capability of shifting energy, you are chosen for the action.

It is with much love and praise that we offer these words. Go forth now and deliver. It is your turn.
With love forever the Teachers.

ACTING OUT ON THE BEST RULES

Now is the time to consider the likelihood of your continued love and support of Earth. Now is the time because you can think and act while in body on Earth. Oh we in spirit can think, but we can't act in the way you can. Therefore, it would be our joy to have you act for us in peace and joy. Act as if you are the savior of Earth. Act on behalf of all the joy on Earth and beyond. Act out and become a spectacle of joy for everyone to see. And if anyone asks about your acting out, ask them to join you in the movement of peace.

We invite you to move physically in the direction of peace. To move means to dance, embrace, sing, hug, smile, and be. Be in joy for no particular reason. Be in joy just because you can and because you have a physical body to express your joy. Practice being spontaneous with your happiness. You don't have to wait for an event which creates joy in you. No reason is necessary other than you can. The best rules to live by are the rules of joy, love, and happiness. Those are the rules which are timeless. The best rules you can live by are infinitely better than all the others.

ANY QUESTIONS?

Let's state the obvious. It seems as though we have made your purpose and your role very clear. Do you question our messages? Do you question your abilities? Can you see the simplicity in living a loving life? Is it clear that if you are in tune to the loving part of yourself, all of forever will prosper? For now, this seemingly simple way of being may sometimes be difficult. It will take awareness and practice. Eventually, in the not too distant future, living peacefully will be the habit of Earth's life forms. You are the beginners of peace. The path has been laid and now is the time to move in the direction of a surviving, loving planet. Other planets in the vastness of space await the completion of Earth's journey. Other life forms will be visiting once the job is complete.

I think we have been very clear. I think that if you have further discussion; communicate with your heart space. Take time to listen to the energy that passes through you, and take the time to talk with each other. Know that we will always be here and talking with you. Your job is to move the mountains of energy; our job is to show you the way. Sometimes it was your job to show the way and sometimes it was our job to move the energy. You and we are one. One energy for love, for life for always.

EARTH SUCCEEDED INTO THE NOW

This is the time to let you know that Earth has succeeded. It is now passing through the realm of negative power and into the realm of positive power. For that, everyone can give thanks. Have celebrations. Have many celebrations for the positive energy of love/life on earth. It is no longer time to imagine, it is time to experience the love, peace, and joy within. We celebrate you, we applaud you. Earth has evolved from the one cell to the energy of all that is- love/life. Congratulations Earth. We applaud you.

186

And yes, we recognize the struggles, the unnecessary tortures and deaths. We know the times were difficult on a prosperous planet which abandoned each other. We recognize a loving planet who failed to love and accept because of negative energy. Those days are gone. NOW is the time to wake up to prosperity. In every aspect of your life, there is prosperity by natural law. Only the human law changed the prosperity to fit some but not others. Wake up. There is enough for everyone and enough love to engulf all of life and beyond. This is the land of plentifulness. Live as if. Live as if you have enough of all. You do. NOW stop the thought of hoarding prosperity. Let it flow. There is an endless flow if you will allow. It is FEAR from the past that created the attitude and energy of hoarding. Let it go. Release and let enough flow to everyone. Become a part of the NOW.

GROWING TOWARDS THE FUTURE

We the Teachers want you all to know that you are the energy of tomorrow. You are the future of the planet. It is your Energy that will guide life on earth forward or will diminish life on Earth. Everyone is responsible. Everyone radiates energy. Blaming one person or one leader is adding to negative energy. Blame is negative and it avoids personal responsibility. You are personally involved in the energy of the whole. You are the god, the source, the whole of all that is. You can't give away your power, but you can refuse to accept it. Yet, why would you? Why would you pass on your ability to express your infinite love, your power within, your greatness and your strength? Is it fear? Is it doubt? What is it about your negative energy that you are holding on to instead of releasing for your greatest energy?

Once you tune into your greatest, farthest reaching, most clear and unpolluted energy, your existence will change and so will the existence of all around you. Your life will change and so will the life of earth and its future. All you have to do is tune into your joyfulness, celebrations, love, and laughter. Yes, do this no matter your current situation. You can make the current situation better or worse depending on the energy you use. And while you are choosing an energy, know that you, as a life form, will always be connected to the love of forever. Nothing can break your connection of life to life; of love to love. Each incarnation brings you closer to the realization that you are forever. You, as a spirit in physical body, are growing towards your beginning of pure, unpolluted, love. You are growing towards the energy of forever and the future of earth.

THE ENERGY OF THE TRANSITIONER

It is time for everyone to know that Earth is in transition. You are the transitioner. What will be your energy? Will it be the positive energy of love and life or the negative energy of fear and death? As always, the choice is yours and the time is yours. NOW, while you are in physical form, you are transitioning the Earth with the energy you use. Consciously or unconsciously, you are creating negative energy of harm, hurtfulness and death, or creating positive energy of love, joyfulness, and life. Wake up. Become aware of your contributions. How often do you laugh, smile, and create fun? How often do you frown, complain, and create anger? Pay attention to your energy and your contributions to forever, infinite love, god, source, energy of the whole. You are the contributors, the generators of energy to the whole. You are valued because of your abilities, your strength, and your purpose.

Now the choice is yours. You have our words, what are yours? Do you accept or challenge. Either way is acceptable, and either way has a result. You have all the time in forever to find your way to infinite love, the love of forever, source, god. By any name you will feel the difference. We are with you all the way. There is nothing but love from us- through all of your journeys. You are transitioning with earth.

UNDERSTAND WHERE YOU ARE GOING

Let this be the time to consider your fate, your destiny, your purpose. It is your turn to discover the shortest, quickest path to where you are fated to be in the end. Your destiny is to become one with source, god, infinite love Your purpose is to discover the paths back to your beginning, then merge with that beginning- not as a spiritual form, but as one with the whole. You will. Everyone will. Meanwhile, your spirit is in physical body to understand love and the lack of love. In other words, to discover what it would be like to have, and be a part of, a loving whole of all that is, or to have the loss of all that is. Your spirit is here in body for the experience and for the choice. If you became consciously aware of these choices, which way would you choose? Love-Life or Fear-Death. We are giving you an awareness of your choices so that you can live your life accordingly.

This is your confirmation that you are in charge of your future and the future of earth. Do you find this more exciting and less fearful? We hope so. We hope that you will be better prepared to brush negative energy aside and live a more positive life. To be clear, a more positive life means to laugh more, love everyone, smile, feel joyful, be silly and celebrate often. This is our message. Understand where you are going and why you are here.

THE VIEW IS SPECTACULAR

Now, let us say that you are ready for this mission. Wherever you are on your journey and whatever you presently believe to be true, everyone's mission is the same. The best idea would be to not fight, argue, or judge each other. The best idea would be to accept each other's experiences as a personal path; a path that your spirit has already taken or will take in another life time. All the lessons are the same yet the experiences of learning them are different. From our view, everyone on earth is participating in the experiences of learning their path to infinite love. Everyone in physical form chose to be in the experience. No one was coerced no one was forced.

The good news is that now all spirit energy in physical body- that includes animals and plants, will lead earth to peace. In the future everyone will see and experience the result of your experiences and your spiritual growth. You are on a mission. The Time Is Now. The View Is Spectacular.

YOU ARE THE PEACE MAKER

Now, it is time to say that the words we give you are meant to be used as a guide for a prosperous, loving, healthy life. These words are for your benefit. They come at a time when the world is in transition. As Earth transitions into peace, it will be the people who provide the positive energy. Yes, of course the plants and animals will also, yet it is the energy of the people who will be making the shift. The movement is in place and the energy of earth is changing. Know that the chaos will bring about the change into peaceful awareness. We suggest that you don't focus on chaos; focus instead on the healing outcome. Even though you may not be able to see the outcome until it arrives, you *can* see with your heart space. Your love will guide you to the visions you wish for. Be assured that now is your time to participate in the transition to a loving planet. You are the dream maker. You are

190

the energy behind the movement. Begin now to accept and participate in the changes.

This is an exciting time for planet Earth. We hope you all will enjoy the excitement and joy that has already begun. Now is your time, now is the time for Peace on Earth. You are the peacemaker and you will do this through your love, joy, and happiness. Allow this to be.

YOU ARE IN CHARGE, WE ARE THE MESSANGER

There is no need to look further than the love within. You don't need to search for a special "someone" out there to fulfill your desires. You don't need an out-there god, or an out-there lover. All the answers and all the love are within you. All you need is to tune in. We understand that many of you don't know how to do this. Well, the answer is not in your brain- never will be. The answer is in your heart space; your connection to all that is. That means you will need to listen to your daydreams, maybe your night dreams, your intuition, your conversations with self.... Or possibly seek out a person who *can* hear within for you. Of course the other person may not speak YOUR truth, so weigh their words. Does it feel right, does it resonate with your truth? Do you have doubts? Keep searching until you get the sigh of relieve that says, "This is right for me at this time." Keep in mind that what is right in one time may change in a different time. Therefore keep searching for the truth within. Work towards your ability to hear, see, and experience the truth within. That means, try to connect your five senses to your spirit. In the beginning of time on earth, everyone could do this; plants and animals still can. It is humans who have deviated from the path. In the deviation, the "brain" came up with lots of new ideas- that work for some but not for all. It is time to get back on the path of survival for all of Earth. It is time now before all of Earth is destroyed by negative energy. Have we made ourselves clear? You are in charge, we are the messenger.

STAY POSITIVE DURING THE CHANGES

There are episodes of this evolving peace. There are times of change followed by a brief recess then another, different time of change. One occurrence will follow the next. This will be the process until the changes are complete. All changes will be for the betterment of all earth. Therefore, many changes will not be popular by the few who hold the majority of what everyone else wants and needs. The time has come for equality of life on earth. We are pleased with the new view. We are pleased to see that the abundance of earth will be shared by everyone. No one will be hoarding and no one will be left out. Now is when the changes are being made to include everyone. Of course the changes may look like chaos yet the chaos is necessary to show the differences. Once the differences are understood, actions will take place to bring alignment. Know that all is a part of a larger change.

And now accept that you all will be participating in one way or another. Everyone will have their role. Many people will come to earth and die for the cause of peace. They agreed before the coming to shed light on the movement. View the changes coming in good time, and allow the movement. Allow peace on earth to evolve from the chaos and negative energy. As much as you can, focus on staying positive. Stay with loving energy for all of earth.

EXPAND INTO ENDLESS TIME

Now we want to talk about time. It is clear to us that time on Earth is different than time in infinite space. In spirit, in space, there is no measuring instrument. Time is not measured with a clock, calendar, or measuring stick. Your linear thinking is not important outside of Earth. We would like you to imagine non-linear thinking. If you can think non-linearly, can you feel the difference? The feel is more like swirling in the vastness of time. Imagine the swirls being energy that goes on infinitely. Without a body, it is possible to ride these swirls of energy to anywhere you would like to be. All that is necessary is to create the desire. Everyone has the ability to do this and everyone does it whether or not they are aware. Traveling through time is something that is easy to do during a day dream. It's also done during hypnosis, which is really a relaxed state like a day dream.

The reason we talk about this is to let you know that anyone can travel through time. All that's necessary is a relaxed state and a desire. We think that now is a good time to develop awareness of your time travels. Practice noticing your daydreams, your reminiscing, and your times of zoning out. See where your thoughts and your desires are taking you. Develop consciousness of time travel and expand your ability to experience life outside the present. Know that you are a part of always and you still have access to always- but not through the five senses. Expand into endless time, endless peace, and endless love.

ALLOW THE PATH TO PEACE

It is clear to us that the people on Earth are coming together as one planet. It is clear that in the end, everyone will live in harmony. The path is available, many are walking on it, and many more will be joining. Although the view of Earth has many mixed colors of light energy- which means many different emotions, the outcome will be towards the colors of positive energy. When this happens, Earth will be at peace and the life forces will be in harmony. It will happen.

For now, stay aware of your own energy. Practice knowing the energy that you are putting out into the world and beyond. Expand your joyful loving self and decrease you fearful, tearful, angry self. You are here now to create the change towards a peaceful planet. It is your contributions which will create the differences. Know of your power, your strength and your endless loving connection to all that is. You are valuable and now is your time. Know also that the more positive energy you put out, the more peaceful and positive your own life will be. Allow this truth to be. Allow YOU to be.

A FLOWER IN THE DESERT AND A CRYSTAL IN THE SNOWFLAKE

We will write now about the images of peace. It's time to visualize again. This time we ask, can you imagine or see a vision of peace? What would it look like to you? What would it feel like? You can imagine the look and feel of prosperity for everyone. You can imagine that everyone is connected to the love within. You can imagine your physical world- a glow in peaceful light. Those are just a few views of the peaceful earth. There can be millions of other views. Each person can have their own view, and can share the views of others. Now is a good time to start the viewing. When you do, the world will change. The changes will follow the energy of your world view.

We suggest that you stop viewing the problems and focus more on the preferred peaceful, beautiful, view of a loving planet. View from your heart space. Look for what you want to see. Desire the look and the feel of a loving prosperous planet. Focus on it, and the view will appear. There is a flower in the desert and a crystal in the snow flake. Look for it; enlarge the view, live from the beauty, live from your heart space. Create the views in your mind so that they can materialize in your world.

WE ARE THANKFUL FOR THE TEAM PLAYERS

We want you all to know that the future of Earth is in your control. This isn't a threat, it is a blessing. We are all thankful for your contributions of loving concern. Yes, we feel an enormous concern from the life on earth; we belief that the vast majority of life wants the continuation of life. That isn't surprising since everyone came from love/life, and everyone is still connected and will return to love- even the cockroach. Sometimes though, struggles get in the way and change the decisions and outcomes. It is more important than ever to know that your struggles are of human kind, not of spiritual kind. You are a spirit in physical body. Your spirit will outlive your body. Go with your strongest self. Tune in to both, they work together, and don't exclude one for the other. Break the habit of excluding your spirit- your connection who sees the bigger picture. Be a team.

BREAK THE RULES AND BECOME ONE LOVE ONE LIFE

Now, we want you to know that you are the deal makers, the rule breakers, the saviors of yourself and of earth. Your energy is why earth will survive or perish. Each of you individually is contributing to the energy of earth and the energy of all. Be conscious. Develop awareness. Become enlightened to your purpose of expanding light, positive, energy.

What more do you want to hear about your purpose? Do you understand your purpose? The Now Books have one message- the message of love. Peace, joy, happiness, laughter, grins, smiles, and hugs are all indicators of love. We are asking you all to live from this place. It will get easier as time goes on, for now continue to practice frequently. You have the ability and you have the information. Now all you need is desire. Desire the best, and break with the negative rules. Let go of judgments, separations, blaming, and anger. Become one world, one planet, living in one love. Live in the love of forever, and live in the love of life.

THE RIGHT ENERGY IS POSITIVE

These Now Books are a reminder of my true message which is and always has been of infinite love. Start with yourself, and then allow your love to spread outward. That is the only way. Become in physical form, that which you are made from. You see, it doesn't do any good to come from love and deliver fear. Your physical body, physical mass, has the ability to move the energy of love. Use your body for the purpose of its design. In time, all life will go back to the energy of peace. You can begin now to change the flow of the last few thousand years. The healing will happen when the energy is right. The right energy is positive. Let it be.

NOW IS YOUR TIME AND YOUR PLACE

Right now, where you are, this place in your time is the perfect environment for creating the changes. The changes you create will be your mark on all of forever. We want you to know that you are the carriers of the truth. You are the ones who will deliver the peace. You have the words you have the physical bodies to move the energy of your desire. You, who have learned the words, will set the pace for others until eventually, everyone walks in peace, love and prosperity.

We also say this is the beginning of a new way for the life of earth. This planet is your paradise, your heaven, and your home. With clean, loving energy, it will survive. We welcome you as the

196

voice and the action for the new Earth. Now when you hear the words Peace On Earth, you will know it is an energy that you have the power to produce. You are the generators of Earth's energy. Its future will align with your purpose.

Now is your time and your place. Use these words to know that you are a part of infinite love. You are no more and no less than we the Teachers. We are all one, we come from one, and we will always be a part of one source. We all are the source of love and life.

In the next book, The Book Of Infinite Love, we will explain more of what you can't see but are a part of. We will talk about the energy of all that is.

With love forever,

The Teachers with Lauren

Your Notes.

Your Notes.

www.ingramcontent.com/pod-product-compliance
Lightning Source LLC
LaVergne TN
LVHW091216080426
835509LV00009B/1029